To Hear God's Word, Listen to the World

The Liberation of Spirituality

William Reiser, S.J.

Paulist Press
New York / Mahwah, N.J.

Book design by Brett Hoover, C.S.P.

Cover design by Moe Berman.

IMPRIMI POTEST:

Very Rev. William A. Barry, S.J.
Provincial
Society of Jesus of New England

Scriptural quotations are taken from the *New Revised Standard Version Bible*.

Library of Congress Cataloging-in-Publication Data

Reiser, William E.
    To hear God's word, listen to the world : the liberation of spiritu-
    ality / William Reiser.
      pm. cm.
    Includes bibliographical references.
    ISBN 0-8091-3696-1 (alk. paper)
    1. Spiritual life—Catholic Church. 2. Liberation theology.
    3. Catholic Church—Doctrines. I. Title.
BX2350.2.R435 1997
248—dc20   96-29367
                                            CIP

Published by Paulist Press
997 Macarthur Boulevard
Mahwah, New Jersey 07430

Printed and bound in the
United States of America

Contents

Dedication

For the members of Saint Luke the Evangelist Parish in Westboro, Massachusetts, and their pastor, Father George Lange, who graciously invited me to deliver the series of winter lectures which became the basis of this book.

Well, now at fifty, I cannot say that I have never been disillusioned. But neither can I say that I yet share the poverty and suffering of the poor. No matter how much I live in a slum, I can never be poor as the mother of three, six, ten children is poor (or rich either). I can never give up enough, I have always to struggle against self. I am not disillusioned with myself either. I know my talents and abilities as well as failures. But I have done woefully little. I am fifty, and more than half of my adult life is passed. Who knows how much time is left after fifty. Newman says the tragedy is never to have begun.

—Dorothy Day

"Where there is no vision, the people perish," can be translated in slightly different ways. Another translation says, "Where there is no prophecy, the people will cast off restraint." The bitter meaning of that sentence has become painfully clear to me now, right in my own neighborhood. When vision is lacking, people quickly degenerate into their worst selves and begin behaving in violent and destructive ways.

—Jim Wallis

In the morning, while it was still very dark, he got up and went out to a deserted place, and there he prayed. And Simon and his companions hunted for him. When they found him, they said to him, "Everyone is searching for you" (Mk 1:35–37).

Introduction

However rational, however compelling, however logical the arguments for Western unity may be, however obvious the benefits of economic co-operation, however hopeful the promise of amity between the nations, one may still question whether reason or logic, of itself, is enough to change the direction of Western development. The vitalities that must be mastered are the fiercest in the world. They appeal to the ultimate instincts of mankind—the protection of the tribe and the struggle for physical survival. Reason may be outmatched in its struggle with such giants. Has Western man other forces to summon to his aid?

—Barbara Ward, *Faith and Freedom*

Well, now we are going to talk a little about the Assembly of God. They have a lot of problems. They judge one another among themselves, and they say they are the best. They pray with wordiness and shouts to be heard by God. I took an opportunity to ask a member of the church why they shout so much and roll about on the floor to pray to God. He told me that they shout a lot and roll about on the floor and bang themselves a lot so that God will pay attention to them. They say that they are only heard by God

1

through the shouts and blows since God is disgusted to the point of indifference because of the many sins of humanity. For that reason they use force to get God to listen. But as a consequence of the shouts and the blows, three of the members of this church became mentally ill.

—*Ignacio: The Diary of a Maya Indian of Guatemala*

Some years ago on the second or third day of a student retreat, a frustrated young man asked me to teach him how to pray. The whole exercise of praying seemed futile to him. Thinking, reflecting, examining his conscience were activities he could do. But when it came to relating himself to God, he was getting nowhere. Noticing the other students wrapped in tranquility with their bibles at their side and sitting meditatively in front of the blazing fireplace or on the rocks by the shore, he felt both cheated and isolated.

I immediately thought of the episode in the gospel when the disciples asked Jesus to teach them how to pray, and he offered them what came to be called the Lord's Prayer. But that desperate student was not looking for the right words to use; he was looking for an experience. Generating experiences of God, however, is not something one person can do for another. Other Christians can help us notice and clarify what is going on interiorly, but they cannot have our experiences for us. The reports we hear of people being moved by the deep faith and aura of the divine surrounding visionaries, like the children who claimed to have seen Mary at Fatima or Medjugorje, confirm just how much we count upon one another's faith and devotion. But vicarious experiences of God are unsatisfactory. Besides, visions are never short-cuts to deeper prayer, and they are not granted in order to reassure individuals about the existence of God. Genuine visionary experiences proceed from faith; they do not cause faith where it did not already exist to a remarkable degree. All of which means that people with little or no faith are not going to experience visions of God, or Mary, or any other heavenly messenger.

The more the student and I spoke, the more I realized that what I had always taken for granted about prayer, namely, that in prayer one simply speaks to God and that anyone with an ounce of faith can do this, was a colossal assumption. There are spiritually earnest people, I was discovering, whose minds get tangled and frustrated when they attempt to talk to God, whether they use their own words or whether they borrow words from a prayerbook or a bible. For such people, there may be more interior satisfaction in addressing the stars or the ocean than in formulating words for God to hear. After all, God "hears" infinitely more than any one of us could manage to say in an entire lifetime. The fact that we do not say something does not mean that God does not hear what is churning in the silent depths of our minds and hearts. God hears us, even if we can do no more than address the stars. But such a theologically beautiful conviction may provide little consolation for an individual who is struggling to pray and to experience a living contact with God.

Please do not misunderstand me. I firmly believe that every human being exists in relation to God and that each human being is capable of growing in that relationship. But I do not believe that every human being prays the same way. Furthermore, I think we have to be very careful as we instruct others about prayer not to suggest that praying is like carrying on a conversation with an imaginary friend, or even like conversing with a real friend who is present but not visible.

None of us would ever propose, of course, that prayer

is a matter of conversing with an imaginary person. We conveniently get around that by substituting faith for imagination. Prayer, we would insist, is a *faith* relationship with a *real* person, and we naturally employ our imaginations in the service of that belief. Yet some people simply cannot escape the icy suspicion that prayer is *only* an exercise of imagination. They want more from prayer, but they do not know what to do. What might Jesus have suggested if the disciples had asked, "Lord, help us to believe in God"? Would he have urged them to ask for a vision as a way of jump-starting a prayer relationship with God?

And prayer is not a matter of pretending that God is really present but not visible, like someone sitting on the other side of a screen, or even like a phantom which communicates with the living through various physical means. The reason we do not see God is not that human eyes are physically incapable of perceiving what exists in the realm of the spirit. After all, the same physical limitations would apply to all our senses. We are equally incapable of hearing and even tasting God, despite the psalm's invitation, "O taste and see that the Lord is good" (Ps 34:8). The reason we cannot see God is that we exist *in* God, not *outside* of God. It might make better sense to compare God to the eye itself, the faculty by which we look at the world and without which vision would be impossible. God and the believer are not identical, but neither are they like distinct objects which exist alongside one another, or like two individuals seated in opposite chairs.

Suppose, however, we defined prayer differently. Instead of thinking of it as a conversation with God, suppose we tease our minds and think of prayer as *a conversation with God's people*, whose company is an indispensable condition for experiencing God in our time. What this might mean is something we shall have to look at, but at

least as an opener we could appeal ι
number of religious figures. Consider:

What do both Moses and the Budd.
mon? To begin with, both were princes; the ι
was a king, and Moses, having been adι   ιne
Pharaoh's daughter, was raised in the royal   ιsehold.
Outside the protection and security of the palace gates, the
young Siddhartha Gautama encountered human misery for
the first time, and that encounter precipitated his great conversion to the contemplative life.[1] One day, after he had
grown up, Moses came across some of his Israelite kinsmen
in forced labor and saw an Egyptian strike one of them,
and he killed the Egyptian. Moses' encounter with violence
and injustice led to his flight from the Pharaoh's palace and
marked the start of his career as a liberator and man of God.[2]

Or better yet, what do Charles de Foucauld, Mother
Teresa and Thomas Merton have in common? Each of them
had entered religious life, yet during the course of their
lives as religious they encountered something which
turned their vocations inside out. Charles de Foucauld had
joined the Trappists. But one day, coming across a terribly
poor Syrian family that lived just outside the monastery
gate, he realized that his own poverty as a religious could
not compare to the misery being endured by that family,
and he felt himself called to something deeper, to a closer
identification with the poor and marginalized tribal
nomads of North Africa.[3] Mother Teresa tells of the
moment when she stepped outside her convent gate in
Calcutta and encountered a dying man in the street. That
moment marked the beginning of her conversion to a profound solidarity with the poor and the dying of India and
the whole world.[4] And Thomas Merton wrote of his experience in downtown Louisville when he suddenly realized
that all the people on those city streets somehow belonged

to him and he to them.[5] In each case, the experience of solidarity with others caused a reassessment of life and led to a different sort of faith, a different contemplative vision, even to a different sort of practice.

I mention these figures because the lives of men and women in religious life often serve as laboratories of Christian spirituality. Their discoveries are meant to be shared. Their experience of God has implications for the way the rest of us make our way in the world as people trying to pray and practice our faith, while their insight into the workings of the human heart are as much for our benefit as for their own.

In the following pages, I want to explain what I believe to be an axiom of the interior life. Oneness with God necessarily entails solidarity with the world; oneness with God in Christ necessarily involves solidarity with communities of suffering, the crucified peoples of every time and place. Much of what is taking place in Christian theology and spirituality today, particularly in terms of what is known as making "the preferential option for the poor," is a corrective of past neglect of the solidarity aspect of religious experience. I do not mean that as a church we failed in love and service of the neighbor; we have not. We may not have always attended to the way justice and faith mutually determine each other, but no one can fault us for having been blind to the needs of men and women in distress.

What I mean, then, is that God and the poor belong much more closely together than we have imagined possible. Love of God and love of neighbor are really love of God and love of the poor: and these are not two loves, but one. Jean-Yves Calvez writes:

> [T]here is no question of reducing one of the two terms, one of the two loves, to the other—just as one cannot reduce to each other experience of the world

and experience of God. But the unity of the two loves is truly strong, "ontological." It goes beyond implying that the love of God morally requires the love of the neighbor.[6]

Find God, and there we will find men and women crucified by poverty, violence, racism, greed and all forms of injustice. Find the poor and the oppressed, and there we shall find God. That, in a nutshell, is the thesis which I have tried to elaborate in the pages that follow. Such is the lesson I would draw from the preamble to the lives of the Buddha and Moses. The spiritual corrective provided by a deep sense of solidarity is what I find demonstrated in the stories of Charles de Foucauld, Mother Teresa and Thomas Merton. And what happened to them is hardly unique.

A True Development Within Christian Spirituality

It would not be possible to trace here the many currents of thinking, both Catholic and Protestant, which contributed to the basically world-oriented spirituality that has been developing within various Christian communities over the past several decades. On the Catholic side, much of the groundwork for conceiving prayer as a conversation with the world was actually laid by the Second Vatican Council, particularly in its decree *The Pastoral Constitution on the Church in the Modern World*. The opening words of that decree, which might well be the council's most celebrated document, have been quoted again and again:

> The joys and hopes and the sorrows and anxieties of people today, *especially of those who are poor and afflicted*, are also the joys and hopes, sorrows and anxieties of the disciples of Christ, and there is nothing truly human which does not also affect them [No. 1].

Throughout the *Pastoral Constitution* one finds sentiments like the following:

> We are warned that it is of no profit if we gain the whole world but lose ourselves. And yet *the expectation of a new earth should not weaken, but rather stimulate, the resolve to cultivate this earth* where the body of the new human family is increasing and can even now constitute a foreshadowing of the new age [No. 39].

> Christians can have nothing more at heart than to be of ever more generous and effective service to humanity in the modern world. That is why, in fidelity to the gospel and drawing on its power, and *in union with all who love and pursue justice*, they have accepted a vast undertaking on this earth...[No. 93].[7]

For Catholics, Vatican II left no doubt that the church as a praying, believing community had to face the world in a spirit of openness to its achievements and a sense of belonging to its history. Quickened by a hope born of faith in the risen Christ, the church has a mission to persuade the world of God's enduring love. Otherwise the human race might collapse under the weight of devastating social and economic burdens, the challenges posed by emerging technologies, burgeoning populations, and widespread disregard for basic human rights.

Then in 1971 the Second General Assembly of the Synod of Bishops issued a document entitled *Justice in the World*, in which we read:

> Action on behalf of justice and participation in the transformation of the world fully appear to us as a constitutive dimension of the preaching of the Gospel, or, in other words, of the Church's mission for the

development of the human race and its liberation from every oppressive situation.[8]

The conviction expressed here is stunning both for its clarity and for its radicalness. According to this document, there is absolutely no way for Christians to teach and preach the gospel without a firm commitment to the peoples of the world and to reshaping all aspects of human existence so that they reflect God's passion for justice. And since preaching the gospel naturally presupposes an engagement with the living Christ through prayer, the work of justice is not going to come about unless Christians have first discovered the Lord of justice within the gospel story. The way we think and act is going to reflect a profound change in the way that we are learning to pray.

The interrelation of faith and justice, together with what has been called "the preferential option for the poor," has arguably become the driving theological concern of our time. The impact of the faith/justice connection on Christian life, prayer and spirituality has been enormous. The reason for its emergence into such prominence surely has to be the acute awareness among so many Christians of the enormous suffering of millions of people in our world, coupled with a desire to assist in the transformation of those political, social and economic forces and structures which are preventing the vast majority of men and women on our planet from living like sons and daughters of God.

According to *Justice in the World*, the Christian community must constantly refine the practice of justice in its own life, and it must educate men and women to what justice means and what it demands. Education for justice has to be both ongoing and practical:

> Accordingly, this education is deservedly called a continuing education, for it concerns every person

and every age. It is also a practical education: it comes
through action, participation and vital contact with
the reality of injustice.[9]

As the privileged expression of a community at prayer, the
liturgy, the document goes on to say, can be a place where
Christians are educated for justice through catechesis,
reflection on the scriptures and even through the act of
eucharistic worship itself.[10] In the liturgy, it would seem,
prayer and world should come together almost naturally.

But the last words of the above text really ought to be
underlined, for they draw attention to what may prove to
be the hardest challenge for every one of us. What does it
mean to have *vital contact with the reality of injustice*? Is such
a proposal feasible? Is this vital contact recommended for
all of us or just for some? Indeed, is it possible that such
vital contact might be an indispensable condition for the
integrity of Christian prayer in our time?

I suspect that the rhetoric about the inseparability of
faith and justice has been losing a good bit of its passion
and moral energy; the vital, underlying concern gets easily
obscured in harmless religious jargon. Language about
making a preferential option for the poor, however, sounds
immediate and decisive. The Catholic bishops of the
United States wrote in their 1986 pastoral letter *Economic
Justice for All*:

> As individuals and as a nation, therefore, we are
> called to make a fundamental "option for the poor."
> The obligation to evaluate social and economic activ-
> ity from the viewpoint of the poor and the powerless
> arises from the radical command to love one's neigh-
> bor as one's self.[11]

In the years since *Justice in the World* and *Economic
Justice for All* the theme of justice has been a constant

refrain among Christians everywhere. It recurs regularly in the encyclical letters of John Paul II, where the demands of justice are often couched in terms of solidarity, and in periodic statements from episcopal conferences around the world.[12]

Reviewing these documents suggests that something new and religiously exciting has been taking place among us, something akin to a contemporary development of dogma. The current development is not taking place in our understanding of the creed or in our moral principles, however, but in our spirituality. As the concepts of faith doing justice and making a preferential option for the poor have infiltrated our religious sensibilities, we have come to appreciate why good works, even justice itself, are not simply a logical *consequence* of faith. The disposition to act justly and compassionately is the presupposition of knowing and experiencing God in the first place.

If we are true believers, it has often been said, then virtuous acts should flow from us more or less automatically. What we have been discovering in the years since Vatican II, however, is that our experience of God is itself more complex than we realized. God and the neighbor in need—God and the poor—belong intimately together. There is a particular experience of God to be had when one makes the option for the poor. One begins to find God *in the people*. From the viewpoint of religious experience this is quite different from undertaking works of charity, even very heroic works, because one is *motivated* by piety and faith, or the love of God.

In order to have "vital contact with the reality of injustice" or to evaluate economic and social reality from the perspective of the poor and powerless, we shall have to be willing to introduce major changes in our lives. At least in the beginning, some of these changes could well seem very unappetizing. From every one of us, a conversation with the world which is initiated and sustained by faith is going to call for changes in our loyalties, attitudes and commitments, and in the way we identify ourselves in terms of social and economic class. For what is gradually taking hold, I think, is a way of drawing near to God that is far more rooted in history and far more rooted in the gospel than we have been accustomed to. While God and the poor do not simply fold into each other, the route to one inevitably winds through the other.

Spiritual writers have traditionally drawn upon the vast reservoir of humanity's inner experience in order to illuminate the soul's path to God, and even to shed light on the divine mystery itself in its self-communication to us. Their writings usually concentrated upon the interior woman and the interior man, that is, to the individual believer, in the moments of his or her ascent to holiness. There we found mapped out for us the interior path to perfection through the three classical "ways" or "stages" of purification, inner illumination and contemplative union with God.

There is, however, another kind of interiority besides that of the solitary believer before God. We might call it *the interiority of the people of God*. What we encounter there is not the religious experience of an individual Christian so much as the rich historical experience of believing yet suffering humanity. The interiority of the people of God follows in its ascent to perfection a path more ancient than the classical three ways, namely, the way of the cross. But for now the final stage of that way—the resurrection or the "fifteenth station of the cross," which corresponds to the classical stage of contemplative union with God—can only be sketched provisionally in terms of humanity's burning, confident hope for a world fully redeemed. The already/

not-yet character of Christian existence applies above all in the case of history's suffering ones, for they live in sometimes desperate, sometimes joyous expectation of the world's definitive liberation. Contemplative oneness with the divine will never be completely possible in this life for any one of us so long as so many men, women and children languish in oppressive and dehumanizing conditions. Christian interiority today is starting to reveal the markings of a different religious landscape.

And the Word Became World

In light of the great numbers of studies of Jesus and the gospels in the last few decades, one conclusion appears to be inescapable. We cannot have a *real* Jesus Christ located in an *unreal* history. Real people have real histories, and that must include the One whom God has raised from the dead. The problem for many of us was that Jesus had ceased to have a real history and, by virtue of his ascension to God's right hand, had entered the timelessness of God. That belief, in effect, removed Jesus from history; meeting him was like encountering someone in a twilight zone.

New Testament scholarship has given us a very helpful approximation of the actual historical situation in which Jesus lived. We are continually learning more about the social and political background of his ministry and the circumstances of everyday life in first-century Palestine. The difficulty this raises for Christian spirituality, however, is that the actual historical situation of Jesus is not all that relevant to most of us, who have come on the historical stage some twenty centuries later. I hardly mean to overlook the structural analogy between the economic and social oppression which existed in the time of Jesus with situations of injustice which exist in our world today.

Rather, I only mean to point out the obvious fact that our world is not peopled with Roman emperors, scribes and Pharisees, toll-collectors, shepherds, lepers, the demon-possessed and so on.

In recent years, many of us have learned to pray and relate to a Jesus who feels to us both human and historical. But to insert, by means of imagination, the Jesus to whom we address ourselves in prayer back into the first century would be tantamount to returning an *unreal* Jesus to an actual though very distant history. I say an "unreal Jesus" because the historical figure of Jesus is, when we think about it, not the one to whom we pray. The Jesus pictured by devout imagination only appears historical. Christians address themselves to the Jesus who has been raised from the dead, the glorified Christ. Not even the evangelists felt constrained to reproduce and preserve for all time Jesus' own historical moment. They narrated their accounts in ways that made Jesus "speak" to the life and situation of a later day.[13]

What is the solution then? In order to link the Jesus of our faith and prayer with a real history we must turn to the poor and oppressed of history: "For you always have the poor with you" (Mk 14:7). The poor are our link with the gospel story. The first-century history which provides the narrative backdrop for the gospel story becomes real when we connect it with actual histories today, and the unreal Jesus becomes real inside the history of people today who are oppressed and poor. The Jesus who dwells within our imagination, transforming ancient gospel texts into contemporary words of life, is someone truly alive. But he lives pre-eminently in the history of his brothers and sisters in need. This form of *real presence* has important ramifications for Christian spirituality today; it is going to take time for us to fully comprehend and appreciate them.

Since the fourth and fifth centuries the Christian community's teaching about Jesus Christ has been framed in terms of the divine and human natures. Needless to say, whatever we know about Jesus' divinity is refracted through his humanity. But the phrase "human nature" can sound too much like a timeless abstraction, something so universal that it loses all social, cultural and historical definition. As a result, the very things which distinguish Jesus from all other men and women and which render him unique by virtue of his time and place on the world stage have tended to blur.

Perhaps today that ancient teaching should be recast in terms of the divine and the historical. For the primary word of God is human history in its entirety, of which scripture is for us a privileged expression. Indeed, scripture has become for us the key by which we read and interpret the non-biblical word of God. But it is important to remind ourselves that God speaks to us through the breadth of the whole human story, and not solely through the biblical tradition. The Word of God does not merely become flesh; it becomes historical, and in a profound sense it becomes world.

According to the 1971 synod document, an indispensable condition for the preaching of the gospel today is action on behalf of justice and participation in the transformation of the world. The document does not explain exactly why these two things are a "constitutive dimension" of God's good news, except to suggest that salvation which did not include liberation from *every* form of oppression would be woefully incomplete. At the risk of venturing too far, might we say that works of justice belong centrally to preaching the gospel because concern for socially oppressed and economically marginalized people is a constitutive dimension of the holy mystery of God?

If we are on the right track here, then the thirst for God in our time has a somewhat different character from the thirst experienced by generations before us. And one indication of this difference is that in order to satisfy this age-old thirst we shall first have to tread through a very different kind of desert, namely, the wilderness of widespread poverty and human suffering. Neither the Israelites whom Moses led out of Egypt nor Moses himself ever made it to the promised land; their children did. Let us hope, therefore, that the wilderness through which we must walk will not claim so many of us. For those who do make it through will be bearers of the promise: men and women with faith renewed and hope reborn because they encountered the God whose history is inseparable from his people.

One recent summer afternoon an older man in the neighborhood came by to ask whether it was possible for a layperson like himself to lead a contemplative life in the middle of the city. I replied that I was convinced of it, and that so was Ignatius Loyola who founded the Society of Jesus, and nearly every Jesuit whom I had ever known. He then confided that his own prayer life was very dry and had been so for five years.

"It used to be," he said, "that I could find God easily. I would sit in his presence quietly, loving him, and him loving me. Now there is nothing." He paused long enough for what he had just related to register with me. Then he asked, "What should I do? How should I pray?"

The stock answer came easily. I pointed out that many people had experienced rhythms in their prayer life alternating between "consolation" and "desolation," joyful peace and exasperating dryness. Sometimes the dry, desolate periods lasted for years. We talked about that, briefly, although I had the sense that he had heard all of this before. Finally he asked me if I could not think of anything else to say, something which might encourage him as he continued waiting for the return of that familiar experience of "loving him, and him loving me."

"Well," I replied, "there is one other possibility. It occurs to me that God might be drawing the church into a new spiritual plateau. Not just one or two of us, but many people. This plateau is an inner space where we shall never again be able to sit alone with God in that old, familiar way. What we may be discovering, ever so gradually, is that millions of others have invaded our inner space, and that if we are going to sit with God any longer as Christians it will only be together with all of our sisters and brothers, especially with those who are being beaten and nailed by poverty and injustice."

I explained that there could be no going back to "God and me" in the privacy of *my* heart or the solitude of *my* cell or the undisturbed quiet of *my* favorite chapel. The poor will always be there, because where we find God, there we shall find God's people; and where we find God's people, there we shall find God. Maybe the desolation and dryness which sincere people, like himself, are experiencing today is no ordinary rhythm in the spiritual life, but a sign, and indication, that God is drawing the church to a different experience of prayer. This is no ordinary desert we are passing through. When the world itself becomes a wilderness, our only option is to walk with the people of God.

I had been speaking out of a hunch, sketching a prospect that occupies me much of the time. If that hunch proves to be right, then maybe it will be men and women like him—people who want to live in our cities like contemplatives—who will help the rest of us understand what is happening among us and to welcome it. I frequently repeat to myself the verse of Gerard Manley Hopkins:

> For I greet him the days that I meet him, and bless
> when I understand. [14]

Once we recognize that it really is the Lord, and not some
ghost or some primal fear, who is drawing near to us, then
there will be cause for joy. There are days in which I sense
that the world may be turning into a giant wilderness, but
not so much a wasteland bereft of hope as a classroom
where I am being introduced to material I never studied
before.

Shortly before her death in 1943, the French social
philosopher Simone Weil wrote:

> Today an elite will have to kindle the virtue of
> poverty in spirit among the wretched masses. To do
> this it is necessary for those who belong to this elite to
> be poor, not only in spirit, but in reality. Every day of
> their lives they must suffer the pains and humiliations
> of wretchedness. We do not need a new Franciscan
> Order. Monks' habits and cloisters signify separation.
> The new elite must live among the masses and mix
> with them; nothing must come between them. And—
> still more difficult to bear—they must be entitled to
> no kind of compensations; in their relationships to the
> masses about them they must show the same humility
> which a naturalized subject would show to the citi-
> zens of his adopted country.[15]

"Elite" sounds too much like a religious order, and while
religious communities for centuries have rendered invalu-
able service to the church, we need to steer clear of the old
idea that the *highest* gospel ideals could only be realized by
those in monasteries, convents and religious houses. I
would like to suggest, then, that Simone Weil's intuition
beckons all of us at least *to adopt a spirituality* that lands our

minds and hearts squarely among the masses of the world's poor.

I should like to return for a moment to the two excerpts at the head of this Introduction. The answer to Barbara Ward's question "Has Western man other forces to summon to his aid?" has to include the resources of our spiritual tradition. Yet not every spirituality works, as the little story of the Maya Indian from Guatemala demonstrates. Which accounts for why we have to keep thinking about the way we pray, about what happens when we fail to pray in solidarity with suffering humanity, and above all about what happens when we do.

Each of the following chapters looks at a familiar Christian idea from the viewpoint of solidarity with the poor. What ties the chapters together is the claim that praying in the Spirit of Jesus today automatically puts us in contact with the wider world. I have in effect simply combined the religious insight behind two richly suggestive titles, Sebastian Moore's *The Crucified Jesus Is No Stranger* and C. S. Song's *Jesus, The Crucified People*.[16] Most of us would agree that there would be something strange about an interior life that prescinded completely from the gospels and early Christian memories about Jesus. There would be something equally strange about a prayer life in which the world around us absolutely never intruded. The ancient Christian hermit who emerged from his cave after twenty years of solitary meditation and asked who the emperor was and how things stood with the world is no model for Christians living in the Vatican II era.

1

Letting the World Pray Through Us

If we were to ask people who pray regularly what exactly they are doing when they pray, they would most likely answer that they are talking to God. If we were to inquire further as to why they talk to God, their replies would probably take various forms. They may want to voice joy and gratitude over the goodness they perceive in the world and in their own lives, or they may be seeking strength and guidance during difficult times, or they might tell us that they find talking to God relieves a persistent loneliness and insecurity in the bottom of their soul. Prayers have been composed for every imaginable occasion, and these are conveniently collected in prayerbooks and devotional manuals.[1]

Common to all the prayers in such collections, not to mention the prayers which occur in the church's liturgy, is the conviction that prayer is essentially a matter of addressing or speaking with God. Not all praying, however, takes vocal form. Some people enter deep, meditative states which are basically wordless. Depending upon their religious tradition, in such states these individuals experience a oneness with God, or with the Absolute, or with the Spirit, or with Christ; the possibility of union with the divine transcends religious frontiers and confessional differences. Christianity in its various churches and sects, Judaism, Buddhism, Islam and Hinduism are all familiar with the phenomenon of mysticism. By mysticism I mean a oneness with God which pervades the whole of a person's thinking and acting, a oneness which usually goes beyond words and one's conscious attention. I think it could be argued that the surest confirmation of such oneness with the divine has traditionally been compassion.

The New Testament story which perhaps best illustrates the meaning of compassion is the parable of the Good Samaritan, the one whose heart responded to the unlucky man who had been robbed, beaten and left to die at the roadside. The parable, we should point out, is not about doing good in general; it is about rushing to the side of someone in dire need of assistance, namely, "the man who fell into the hands of the robbers" (Lk 10:36). That man represents not merely all those unfortunate enough to have been mugged by petty thieves or desperate addicts on lonely highways or deserted streets; he stands for the countless victims of corporate and national greed, ethnic cleansing and political violence as well.

Jesus' parable suggests a further way of conceiving what prayer is. In addition to thinking of prayer in terms of the human being's becoming attentive or attuned to the divine mystery, perhaps we could also think of praying as the individual's becoming present to the world: and not just the world in an undifferentiated fashion, but the world of the poor and suffering in particular. Needless to say, the world of the poor is not so much a physical place on a map of the earth as a social and cultural space which transcends geographical boundaries. The world of the poor exists in the countries of the north as well as those of the south, in the first world as well as in the third world.

In this chapter we want to explore the possibility that prayer, at least for some people, might more satisfactorily be defined as letting the world speak to God through us. Such a definition assumes two things. First, it presupposes that becoming present to the world in the mode of compassionate listening and responding (or in the mode of solidarity with the oppressed peoples of every time and place) is humanly desirable in and of itself. In the parable of the Good Samaritan, for example, Jesus mentions nothing about the Samaritan's faith or devotion. As a matter of fact, the Samaritan's compassion stands in marked contrast to the supposed piety of the priest and Levite.

Secondly, our definition presupposes that God stands with the world, indeed, that God can be found at its very center in the history of those who are poor and powerless. This conviction can be found in the earliest stages of recorded apostolic preaching. For Paul writes:

> For you know the generous act of our Lord Jesus Christ, that though he was rich, yet for your sakes he became poor, so that by his poverty you might become rich. (2 Cor 8:9)

Christ's becoming poor would make no sense except in terms of his identifying with human beings *in their poverty*. While Paul may be playing on various levels of meaning with the words "rich" and "poor," the phrase *by his poverty* has to refer first of all to Jesus' social and economic location. For Jesus did not share the moral poverty of human depravity, or the spiritual poverty of its fear and despair.

Now let us work out the steps of this definition in a little more detail.

A Dual Starting Point:
John of Damascus and Thérèse of Lisieux

In considering the nature of prayer, Thomas Aquinas enlisted the help of the eighth-century writer John of Damascus. "To pray is to ask fitting things from God," John wrote. And again, "Prayer is the lifting up of the mind to God."[2] In answer to the question "What is Prayer?" the *Catechism of the Catholic Church* turned to the autobiography of the nineteenth-century Carmelite Thérèse of Lisieux:

> For me, prayer is an uplifting of the heart, a glance towards Heaven, a cry of gratitude and of love in times of sorrow as well as of joy. It is something noble, something supernatural, which expands the soul and unites it to God.[3]

The *Catechism* went on to note that properly Christian prayer involves a living relationship or communion which begins with Christ and extends outward until it includes the whole people of God.[4]

Accordingly, we can say at the outset that prayer is above all *other-directed* (Thérèse's "surge of the heart" and "a simple look turned toward heaven"; John's "lifting up of the mind"). It is profoundly *relational* and *personal*, as well as *communal*. And prayer, as Thomas reminds us, is always a *gift*.[5] To paraphrase the *Catechism*, anyone who is truly related to the living God in and through Christ stands by that very fact in relationship to all of God's daughters and sons. A purely private relationship with God is by the very nature of things impossible.

To say that prayer is a gift of God, however, requires some clarification. Is the very ability to pray, that is, to exist in a relationship with God, itself the gift? Or does gift refer to the facility with which we pray, since there are times and moments when the activity of praying can be both difficult and dry? Or is the gift meant to be God's own self which is shared with us when we approach God from the depths of our desire for life and discover in those depths the intensity of God's desiring of us? If so, then what about the person who claims not to be able to pray? Does the inability which such a person feels imply that God withholds the gift from some?

I believe it makes best sense to say that our being in relationship with God—that feature about us which makes us men and women—is already the great gift, like life itself and the creation around us. Everything about us is gift and the first spiritual or interior movement of the heart is wonder, followed by praise and thanksgiving. Prayer then may be a gift. But it is also what human beings do "naturally," that is, according to their nature, whenever they cease looking at themselves and pay attention to the mystery which encompasses them on every side.

From within our tradition there appear to be at least three ways to think about prayer. First, there is *prayer as conversation*. When it comes to prayer, most of us are accustomed to speaking with God or with Christ so simply, directly and personally that we probably would not notice much difference between the way we talk with God and the way we might speak with a close friend. The language of some prayers (for example, the church's eucharistic prayer or the psalms) sounds a lot more formal or even "prayer-like" than the wording of spontaneous, everyday prayer. Yet all Christian prayer, and especially everyday prayer, takes it for granted that God can be addressed, as in a conversation. In fact, prayer as conversation is the most familiar and concise model of prayer that most of us learn. For what else is prayer, except words we say to God?[6] Recalling a moment from his childhood when he overheard his mother speaking, James Melvin Washington writes:

> It was during the early morning hours, while the gladiatorial snores of my sleeping family rebuked silence, that two of us were actually awake. The window of the crowded children's bedroom framed the East Tennessee sky as I lay communing with the stars. A whisper from my parents' bedroom forced me to cease my transporting enterprise. I strained to hear what I would now call a divine soliloquy. It was Mama's voice. She was speaking in piteous hush. I yearn to recapture her exact words. I cannot. I do know that the drama of the moment demanded that I should stop counting stars. I could not resist the temptation to eavesdrop on a most unusual conversation. Mama said a few words about her burdens, anxieties, children. Then an awesome silence would punctuate her lamentation to…God? Who was her conversation partner? Daddy was working on the night shift. "Please, Jesus!" she cried. I felt she was hurt, maybe even dying. I ran to be with her. I rubbed her back while she sobbed.
>
> In many ways I have been in spiritual solidarity with my mother since that moment. She taught me to pray. Her silence and her action taught me that I must pray….Indeed, more than any other, through precept and example, she taught me that prayer is a conversation with God….God is a living, personal presence that is insinuated at all times and in all circumstances.[7]

Second, there can be *presence without conversation*. As we saw above, some Christians have come to the realization that prayer at times can be wordless. There are moments, or even long stretches of our lives, when our relating to God becomes simply a matter of attending to or "resting" in God's presence. We may find ourselves, for example, feeling at a level "too deep for words" (Rom 8:26) glad and grateful for all the goodness which has been shown to us, in spite of our moral failures and even sometimes in spite of great personal suffering. Or we may find ourselves attending to the silent mystery of God, the eyes of our heart fixed on something greater than ourselves and overcome with awe and love at the very thought of that mystery which is both so immeasurably close and encompassing, and utterly transcendent. Whatever the prayer experience, no words at our disposal would be capable of expressing all that is passing through our hearts and minds. But who needs words at such times? Attending to God can be both uncomplicat*ed* and uncomplicat*ing*. Not only is the experience of God basically simple; it also loosens and undoes the knots from the other parts of our lives.

Yet not only can prayer be wordless; it may be largely unconscious. By this I mean that one is dimly aware of the divine mystery, although more in the manner of background music or indirect lighting. When we become overly accustomed to thinking of prayer as a conscious, intentional activity of relating to God, we may not appreciate the pervasive praying which not uncommonly stamps people's experience. I may be praying, in other words, without realizing it. Through all my actions and thoughts, all my spontaneous desires and concerns, my interactions with others and even my body language, through the way I deal with temptation, frustration, anxiety and loss, I am giving expression to the essential reality of my life, namely, my union with the silent mystery of God. John Wright refers to this as "extensive" prayer, and he describes it thus:

> To the degree that God is personally present through-
> out the day as somehow "addressed" by me, I am
> praying always. Normally God cannot always occupy
> the center of one's attention, but God can always be
> there at the periphery, as the atmosphere of one's life,
> to whom one's attention spontaneously returns when
> it is released from other things.[8]

In short, our being in relationship to God does not
pause when we work or when we eat or when we make love
or when we relax with our children; or when, watching the
nightly news, we react with tears and anger over the mas-
sacre of youngsters in a kindergarten in Scotland or a bomb-
ing in Oklahoma or the blowing up of a bus in Jerusalem.
Neither at those moments does our prayer cease. Perhaps
the explanation for this lies close to something Paul wrote:

> Likewise the Spirit helps us in our weakness; for we
> do not know how to pray as we ought, but that very
> Spirit intercedes with sighs too deep for words. And
> God, who searches the heart, knows what is the mind
> of the Spirit.... (Rom 8:26–27)

We shall have reason to return to this text. For now,
the point we wish to draw is simply that *something* (Paul
calls it the Spirit) keeps praying from within us and holds
our spirits oriented toward God, even when in our weakness we are afraid to use the words that will tell the truth
about our lives, or when in our weariness we cannot find
them, or, because we have to live and work, we simply cannot be always attending to God directly.

Third, there is the experience of *prayer as being known*.
In addition to prayer being wordless, there can be another
experience of prayer, an experience which gives rise to a
third definition. For some people, prayer may be better
defined, or described, as *the experience of being known by*

God. This is not to say that these people, unlike the rest of us, never feel moments of gratitude for whatever they have been given. But the sense of having been given good things is not their major *religious* experience. After all, countless people throughout the world have been given precious little, if we measure gifts in terms of things like health, food, security, freedom, economic stability, and so forth. If the awareness of having been richly blessed were the quintessential religious moment of our lives, then the majority of the world would have little reason to develop their relationship with God.

A parallel point could be made about the matter of knowing oneself to be sinful. If the awareness of personal sinfulness were essential to our knowing and experiencing God, then what becomes of all those men and women who themselves are the victims of human greed, pride, fear and callous disregard? It makes absolutely no sense to think that the poor and destitute of this world must learn how to convict themselves of sin before they can receive the healing grace of God. We would not preach to poor widows the merits of almsgiving, or to the famine-stricken the spiritual rewards of fasting. Neither would it make sense to preach repentance to people whose lives have been torn asunder by the sin of others. God, in other words, may be more concerned about healing and making whole than about the sinful state as such. The healing grace which the poor need first might be a plot of fertile ground on which to grow some corn or wheat, or a well with fresh, safe drinking water, or a clinic, or the ability to read, write and vote, or employment, or to be treated with respect and accorded rudimentary justice.

To return to the point, for some people prayer can be characterized as the experience of being known by God: not simply being acknowledged or recognized by God, the way a person might recognize the features of an acquaintance, but known in the sense of being fully and clearly seen by another right down to the deepest, darkest corner of our souls, *and still accepted*. Prayer, in this sense, may feel more passive than active; it appears to be less an activity which we initiate than a movement which we allow to happen. To pray, then, is akin to our being "read" by God. The one who prays thereby lets God take hold of him or her. The praying is no longer a conversation but a being grasped, unfolded and rendered absolutely transparent by a light which is never one's own but the Spirit's.

Lest this sound like an amateur's effort to describe a mystical state, let me repeat that I am not talking about the classical higher prayer states but a third model of what prayer can mean for believers who would not regard their interior lives as the least bit distinguished. The disadvantage of prayer conceived principally as a conversation is that God does not talk back to us the way another person would. God does not speak to us in code through everyday signs, events of nature, accidents, dreams, astrologers, horoscopes, oracles, angels, visions or revelations. The divine redemptive effort or action in dealing with the human race is not a matter of establishing lines of communication. If that were the case, then one could imagine some highly effective, public and convincing means God might take in order to get in touch with us.

It might be more accurate to say, therefore, that God does not have any "problem" in dealing with us, as if we were constantly getting in the way of some mysterious divine outreach and thwarting God's initiatives to contact us. We ought not to think that God is puzzling over ways to make a heavenly message visible, more direct or more comprehensible. Whatever the process of revelation is, it is never a matter of God leaping over a human obstacle course. That is not to say that we cannot at times, like the first disciples, be rather deaf and blind when it comes to grasping the gospel's bearing on our lives. But once our deafness or blindness lifts, the result is not so much that we have clearer access to a God who was previously "hidden," but that our senses are transformed. We see and hear the world in a new way.

What Makes Prayer Christian?

Christian prayer today is more likely to begin, it seems to me, with an experience of the world. Whenever a person turns to God in prayer it is not just God that one finds but other people as well. When we say that the prayer of a Christian grows out of his or her communion with Christ, the name "Christ" refers not only to the individual Jesus, dead and risen, but to the risen Christ who dwells among his followers, the church. To be in union with *that* Christ is to be joined to all believers. Indeed, it is to be joined to all men and women, since all men and women are brother and sister to him. Jesus' saying

> For where two or three are gathered in my name [that is, in prayer], I am there among them (Mt 18:20)

has a reverse side, which is likewise true to experience: wherever Jesus is, or whenever we are with him in the Spirit, there we always find two or three of his sisters and brothers.

The notion of finding "others" with God is hardly new to Christian spirituality. We believe that where the Father is, there too are the Son and the Holy Spirit. Or where the Spirit is, there too are the Father and the Son. The "persons" of God live in undivided unity, as the liturgy for Trinity Sunday reminds us. Should it be surprising then that as Christians we cannot think of the world and God separately? I do not mean to suggest that they are to be identified, as if God were the world, or the world were God. Rather, I mean that one of the key features of our understanding of God has always been God's abiding interest in the human race, and that God, in Jesus, has become intimately and irreversibly a part of our story—God as the one who creates, liberates and redeems, and makes holy moves from within our world.

Christian Contemplation as the Heart's Immersion in the World

Although the prayers we frequently hear at the opening and closing of the eucharistic liturgy seem to place an inordinate stress on the next life, no one can fault them for sounding private or solitary. Clearly, during the liturgy it is the community which prays. By contrast, traditional prayerbooks and devotionals seem to place a heavy emphasis on the individual trying to love and serve God in the particularities of his or her life. Even the short collection *Prayers for a Lifetime* by Karl Rahner, one of the most celebrated theologians of the twentieth century, falls into this mode. Rahner's prayers are theologically precise, careful reflections; they are rooted in common human experience and grounded too in a wonderful sense of church and of fidelity to tradition. Yet how solitary they sound! The self before God, humbly and forthrightly speaking to God its needs, its hope, its sinfulness, its gratitude, its love. Even when the words "we" and "us" appear, they feel unconnected, as if, when all was said and done, salvation (like belief itself) were at bottom a private matter between the individual in his or her freedom, and God.[9]

In marked contrast to Rahner's prayers one finds a book like *Political Holiness: A Spirituality of Liberation*, which was written by Pedro Casaldáliga, the Brazilian bishop well known for his life among the poor, and José-María Vigil, who works in Nicaragua. Political holiness, they wrote, is, among other things,

> a holiness characterized by sensitivity to the majorities in our society, thinking according to the "logic of the majorities," and able to look at them whole, without letting the tree of the individual stop it from seeing the wood of the masses, without being an obstacle, through the assistentialism of aid, to effective justice and charity. This critical sensitivity is able to see the collective poor, not as a mere sum of individuals, but as an organic unit, as a class, as the people, as a marginalized race, as an oppressed culture, a subjugated gender.[10]

While holiness undoubtedly has its vertical dimension, it must contain a horizontal dimension as well. Or perhaps we should say that the model itself needs some correcting. The two dimensions *include* each other. It is not *first* God, *then* the masses of the poor; or even first the masses, then God. Rather, the idea seems to be God *in the people* and the people *in God*.[11]

There are certainly reasons to account for the differences in style and outlook between the piety in the Rahner prayers and the spirituality underlying *Political Holiness*. The solitariness of the Rahner prayers arises, I think, from the fact that in them it is the *individual* who prays. But for Casaldáliga and Vigil, the starting point for thinking about our relationship to God is seen to be our membership among and solidarity with the entire human community, and especially the poor. That starting point is not the individual as such, but the individual as someone in relation to others. To be a bit technical, Rahner's "self" is to a large degree the self of twentieth-century existentialist thought which chooses, decides, acts and loves and thereby actualizes its God-given freedom. But the self's interiority—the dynamics of its inner space—can also be conceived a little differently. The self is not just one; it is many. Its primary achievement in this world is not so much the perfection of its inner freedom through life-giving moral choices as the realization of its solidarity with all men and women, particularly those who make up suffering humanity.

Saint Augustine had a wonderful insight in the matter of praying the psalms. According to Augustine, there are three who pray: the person before God, Christ, and the church.[12] Many times I have read the psalms, trying to imagine how the words would sound coming from the lips of Jesus. As a devout Jew, he surely would have prayed or chanted them often. Yet to imagine *Jesus* reciting the psalms is not the same thing as imagining *Christ* praying them. For the risen Christ is the Christ of the church. He is not an individual in our sense of the term, an independent, enclosed, autonomous self. The risen Jesus—the Christ—dwells among his followers, who are the church. Christ and church are inseparable, and for that reason Augustine's insight requires a little adjusting. It is not just I who pray the psalms, but the whole people of God; and the link which joins us is the risen Jesus, the Christ. Augustine did not express his insight in these terms, but we do him no disservice in saying that the Christian does not pray alone. The Christian always prays, always stands before God, in union with the risen Christ, and thus in union with the whole church.

But what about reversing the idea? If it is not just we who pray, but the whole church praying with us, could we not say that the whole church is also praying *through us*? Again, recall the text from the letter to the Romans:

> ...for we do not know how to pray as we ought, but that very Spirit intercedes with sighs too deep for words. And God, who searches the heart, knows what is the mind of the Spirit....

The sighing "too deep for words" must come from the human heart itself. Paul is telling us that God "reads" our hearts—the deepest desires of our souls—and in them catches the "mind" (or should we say "the desiring"?) of the Spirit itself.

In short, there is another who prays from within us. Suppose that other is Christ. The Spirit given to us is, after all, the Spirit of the risen Jesus. If the other who prays from within us is Christ, and if Christ is always the ecclesial Christ—the Christ who abides among his sisters and brothers—then it seems possible to say that whenever I pray, it is not just I who pray, but Christ who prays in me. And if Christ prays in me, then all those who are with Christ are also praying with me.

Not even Jesus, we might add, would have prayed "alone." When Jesus prayed one of the psalms and repeated words such as

> My, God, my God, why have you forsaken me?
> Why are you so far from helping me,
> from the words of my groaning?
> (Ps 22:1)

he would have been joining his prayer with the fervent voices of countless men and women among his people, as well as with the generations before him. At that point, *me* becomes *us*; welling up from the recesses of his soul were cries and tears from all the rest of God's battered people.

I hope the idea does not sound convoluted or too "logical," as if we were simply drawing out corollaries in a geometry exercise, for the religious point here is almost embarrassingly simple. To claim that when Christ prays within us, all those with Christ are also praying with us reflects an experience, not just a devout abstraction. Furthermore, the idea of Christ praying in us now enables us to look at our third understanding of prayer with new insight. Another approach to prayer, we suggested, is to think of prayer as the experience of being known by God. Yet such prayer can also be the experience of others praying with, in and through us. Their desires and hopes, their suffering and desperation, their poverty and humiliation, their faith and courage are there, within our heart. Their prayer moves, carries and sustains us; their desire becomes our desire. If I am in Christ, then I am always with the poor and crucified ones of history. When Christ prays in me, it is their voice which spills from my lips, their anguish which pours from my heart, and their hope which puts new life into my weakened soul. For a Christian, reading the daily newspaper or watching the nightly news becomes as much an antecedent for prayer as any of the other moments and experiences of our lives.

The Christian, then, no matter how reclusive, never forsakes or leaves the world. Whether they flee to monasteries and deserts, whether they are confined to lonely hospital beds or prisons, whether they are immersed in the countless small but necessary details of daily life, or whether they walk city streets and dwell among the masses of the earth's poor, Christians never abandon the world. Sometimes the experience of being "known" by that world, the experience of others praying in and through us, takes over and we are in God in a way we might never have believed imaginable.

Prayer as Protection Against the Downsizing of God

Most of us would most likely agree that our images and concepts of God are inadequate to the reality of the divine mystery. In the gospel stories, for example, Jesus constantly challenges his listeners with a view of God as being more merciful and forgiving, more generous and loving, than they had ever thought possible. To take another example, Paul's early understanding of divine action in history explodes under the insight that God's saving designs also include the Gentiles. The church today continues to wrestle with the tension between its present grasp of the gospel message and the openness and vision embedded within the gospel texts, for the holy mystery of God can never be neatly defined or contained by sermons, church pronouncements or theological tracts.

Images and concepts of God expand as believers allow themselves to be engaged ever more fully by the world in which they live. It would not be difficult to demonstrate that Jesus derived his message about mercy and forgiveness from his association with those who were technically outside the law and thus "sinners" in the eyes of the righteous. It would be hard to imagine how Paul, a zealous and devout son of Israel, would ever have come to champion the cause of the Gentiles unless he had actually encountered Gentiles as men and women ready to believe in the gospel, that is, unless he had lived among them and interacted with them.

In other words, if we change the circumstances in which we live by dwelling and working among people from a different culture, a different social or economic class, or a different religious background, then we stand a decent chance of being forced to think beyond the categories in which we were raised and schooled, to ask profound questions regarding our common humanity and to reflect on the action of God in our world. I am not likely to think about poor people and the things which make and keep them impoverished if I never meet someone who is poor and let myself become engaged by that person's experience. I am not likely to think about the presence of God in other world religions if I have never entered a Buddhist temple, say, and encountered devout men and women in silent meditation, or if I have never stood in wonder before the religious ruins of an ancient civilization, or if I have no close friends who are Muslims or Hindus.

Our view of God, therefore, is very much influenced by our openness to the world and its concerns. As a matter of fact, the God to whom we address ourselves in prayer is always greater than the picture of God we have assimilated from our doctrinal tradition, and at a deep level of our experience we know this to be true, even if we do not have the conceptual tools or theological skills to explain ourselves. People who live in God's presence, that is, people of prayer, have a sense about the geography of faith. To be people of God ultimately has to mean being with the God of people. The more I allow people to enter my inner world, the more I grow in God.

My reason for developing this point is that we constantly run the risk of reducing or downsizing God to the stature of a literary character. This happens whenever we insist, in effect, upon imprisoning God within the pages of our bibles or within the articles of our creeds, or within the customs and practices of our liturgical and ascetical traditions. Two recent works might serve to illustrate this point.

The first work is Karen Armstrong's *A History of God*,[13] and the second is Jack Miles' *God: A Biography*.[14] Each of these writers draws attention, almost certainly unintentionally, to what we might call the tendency to reduce or downsize God. In the first book, God is made to have a history, like a subject that can be examined within a religious tradition as one might study, for instance, the development of liturgy, penitential practice, social teaching or the theology of grace. In the second, God is considered as a literary character within the "classic" Christian text which is the bible. In the Miles book, it is not God as unseen and incomprehensible mystery who acts in scripture, but God reduced to being an actor within the pages of a wide variety of ancient religious texts.[15]

Now what is helpful about each of these works, I think, is that they render us more sensitive to the language we use when we pray. Are we attempting to speak, in our prayer, with God as silent mystery, or are we addressing God under one of "his" many literary forms? What we know, in other words, or at least what we imagine and relate to when we pray, is sometimes a literary character. The point can be pretty unsettling, especially if we are in the habit of thinking that in prayer we have been addressing God *as God is*.

The fact that we frequently ascribe a personal, masculine pronoun to God should be enough to alert us to the intrinsic limitation of both all language about God and the vocabulary we use as we orient ourselves toward the divine mystery. At the same time, efforts to eliminate gender references from our God-language run up against the same limitation. For the God of our tradition is *both* a literary character *and* the silent, incomprehensible mystery which creates and redeems us.

When God is downsized to the status of a character or

actor in humanity's great religious texts, then what happens? What results, above all, is an infectious uncertainty about the integrity of our religious experience. Is God, after all, merely a literary construction, a creation of human imagination? If this suspicion continues unchecked, then the validity of the doctrines, symbols and practices of our faith will be threatened.

To counter such an attack, religiously motivated people will understandably turn either to *fundamentalism* or to some sort of mystical *inwardness*. Yet these solutions provide at best only a temporary refuge. Fundamentalism for the most part begins in a denial of reality, as if by refusing to think and question and face the demons of modern life we could protect ourselves against an endless night without God. As human beings run for cover against the fearful possibility that the universe has no bottom, they may grab anything that floats by for the illusion of security.

Fundamentalism is essentially a non-prayerful attitude that seeks to erect the finite into something infinite; the history of the world religions is replete with such attempts, especially in the many incarnations of superstition and intolerance. It is non-prayerful because it relates to God out of fear, not out of love and faith; it wants God to be something God is not. There is something profoundly non-prayerful in the militant moralism of Islamic fundamentalism, in the extremism of religious and nationalistic loyalty which led to the assassination of the Israeli prime minister Yitzhak Rabin, and even in the Vatican effort to terminate all discussion of the ordination of women. When the God to whom we relate is no more than a literary character, "he" is all too easily contained. I might *like* such a God, because a God contained never subverts my world; indeed, "he" reinforces it.

Mysticism, on the other hand, particularly in its New-

Age varieties, runs the risk of degenerating into a flight inward where an individual need answer to no one outside himself. Who would presume to question another's profound, intimate experience of the divine? Mystical experience thus becomes privileged and sacrosanct. Moreover, the mystic, as one secretly illumined and loved by God, stands open to the charge of being exclusive or esoteric, since mystical states are not achieved easily but require exercise and training. With work to do and families to support, most people do not have the leisure to devote to such exercises of the spirit.[16] Mysticism may be oriented toward God, but we have to ask if it is genuinely prayerful unless it also embraces the world. Neither a misguided inwardness (which "centers" the world in terms of the self) nor fundamentalism (which centers the self in terms of the finite world) can save us from having to be schooled in the things of God in a way appropriate to our time and place in history.[17]

At the end of her study, Karen Armstrong writes:

> When religious ideas have lost their validity, they have usually faded away painlessly: if the human idea of God no longer works for us in the empirical age, it will be discarded. Yet in the past people have always created new symbols to act as a focus for spirituality. Human beings have always created a faith for themselves, to cultivate their sense of the wonder and ineffable significance of life. The aimlessness, alienation, anomie and violence that characterize so much of modern life seem to indicate that now that they are not deliberately creating a faith in "God" or anything else—it matters little what—many people are falling into despair....
>
> Human beings cannot endure emptiness and desolation; they will fill the vacuum by creating a new focus

of meaning. The idols of fundamentalism are not
good substitutes for God....[18]

Armstrong has identified a major problem: "if the
human idea of God no longer works for us," then we shall
gradually lay it aside. We may outgrow our traditional
understandings of God, she concludes, maybe even outgrow Christianity itself; but we will never renounce religion altogether, because it is through religion that men and
women make sense out of the meaninglessness and violence of their lives and in the world around them.

While Armstrong suggests that modern western societies have lost interest in the traditional God, Miles ends
his book asking whether God might have become disinter-
ested in us. The tragic flaw in the character of God is that
God wants both to be the champion of the poor and powerless and not to intervene in human affairs.[19] This characterization of God certainly corresponds to many people's
experience. Our heads and hearts wrestle with the painful
evils which exist in the world while at the same time we
endeavor to remain people of faith and hope. But the possibility that God might have exhausted the divine concern
for creation and chosen to withdraw into heaven and let
history run its course is truly chilling. Are we headed, at
the close of the second millennium, into a twilight zone of
the spirit? Is the disappearance of the divine mystery from
the human world going to be a matter of mutual consent,
with neither God nor humanity any longer interested in
each other?

And yet, despite all that is happening around us, we
continue to pray. Perhaps at some deep level we realize
that the God of the bible *is* too small for us: we never pray
to Noah's God, who visits the earth with devastating
floods; or to Abraham's God, who orders a father to sacri-

fice his child; or to Joshua's God, who ruthlessly and mercilessly destroys his enemies; or to Moses' God, who takes pleasure in hardening Egyptian hearts; or to Job's God, who toys with the faith of his loyal servants. God, we believe, would not delight in watching the children of his enemies being dashed against rocks (as in Hosea 13:16). We do not even pray to the Father God whom Paul envisions when he writes about the one "who did not withhold his own Son" (see Rom 8:32), and certainly not to a God so wrathful as to destroy innumerable human beings in a giant wine press (Rev 14:19–20).

Even the God of the church can be too small. No one today could credibly argue that God's cause could ever have been the destruction of infidels, or the suppression of truth, freedom and inquiry. We shudder at the crusades, the inquisition and the condemnations of the Holy Office, and we are embarrassed whenever in its history the church tried to enlist God on the side of intellectual, social or technological immobility, or slavery, or cozy alliances with tyrants and dictators. The God of the church has often been little more than a literary character pressed into the narrow service of men who never fully understood the story of Jesus.

Yet in the end we are led to pray because the human soul falls into the silent mystery of God as if by a natural movement, the way particles are drawn to a magnet or the needle of a compass is pulled toward the North Pole. And we continue to pray, because the God of our prayer, at least according to our mind's *intention*, is always larger than our images and ideas about the divine mystery. Whenever we look into a mirror, we expect to see our own face reflected. But when that mirror is God, the face we see is not going to be our own, but that of the poor. This paradox is what ultimately saves spirituality from the trap of self-absorption. In God we shall discover faces we never expected to see.

2

Faith Without Solidarity Is Dead

The insistence that Paul places on the priority of faith over works was the result of his effort to resolve the relationship in the plan of salvation between Israel as God's chosen people and the Gentiles. The fourth chapter of his letter to the Romans, where Paul draws on the example of Abraham, develops the claim that we are justified by faith. The "law of faith" (Rom 3:27) stands contrasted with the works of the law. "For we hold," Paul writes, "that a person is justified by faith apart from works prescribed by the law" (Rom 3:28).

Paul's position seems to confirm the perspective of the gospel. The evangelists severely criticize the Pharisees, who were champions of the works prescribed by the law, for their failure to internalize the spirit of the law, which is faith (for instance, Mt 23 and Mk 7). Time and again, the gospel writers present the Pharisees as Jesus' adversaries who comprehend neither God's mercy nor God's desire to save. On the other side, however, the New Testament also gives us the voice of the letter of James, perhaps as a corrective to any possible exaggeration, which says, "So faith by itself, if it has no works, is dead" (Jas 2:17).[1]

The fact is that none of us would deny the intrinsic relationship between faith and practice. We may speculate

44

about which of the two is logically prior to the other, that is, whether faith precedes good actions or whether right actions are the prelude to genuine faith. But from a Christian perspective, believing and doing naturally fold into one another. Perhaps the ultimate reason for this is that we believe in a God who not merely *is*, but who *acts*. If God's creative and saving action is a natural expression of the divine being, it is also an expression of God's loving oneness with the world. Or to put the idea a bit differently, solidarity is a divine attribute. It points in one direction to what God is (namely, Love) and in another direction to what that Love does (namely, creates, guides, accompanies and redeems). To play off the text from James, perhaps the point could be made more radical by saying that faith without solidarity is dead. For the underlying issue is not one of alternatives (either faith or works), and not exactly one of *both* faith *and* works, since the both/and approach runs the risk of misconceiving the unitary nature of faith. What we need to do is to think of faith in a way that always keeps God and the world together. The idea of solidarity can help us accomplish that.

One of the characters in James Hamilton-Paterson's novel *Ghosts of Manila* confessed:

> Losing your faith is like giving up smoking, I've discovered. You suddenly realise that countless millions are getting by without it and always have done. It doesn't matter. I still wish to live my life well, and for that I need no faith at all. The discovery that wishing to live my life well means helping others to do the same is oddly strengthening and calming. Not praiseworthy; simply logical.[2]

The speaker in this passage is a young priest who has been laboring tirelessly among the desperately poor shanty-dwellers of a barrio in Manila. Later in the story he loses his life while attempting to rescue some children who he thought were caught inside their burning hovel. On a theological level, the priest typifies one of the polarities of Christian faith. In his case, the tension between action and contemplation, between practice and belief, collapsed in favor of complete absorption in selfless service.

The other polarity would be total immersion in the mystery of God, in a mysticism and contemplation that spell total seclusion from the world. As extremes, each of these cases is easily caricatured, and thus easily rejected, as being an inadequate expression of mature Christian faith. Christian faith, one might insist, is more properly to be found in a healthy tension between engagement with the world and one's neighbor, and the desire to be caught up ever more fully in the heart's unquenchable desire for life and love in God.

Yet the mystery of God touches people's lives even at these two extremes. God can appear from within the neighbor, in the thick of the world's messiness, and the neighbor can emerge even from within the mystic's rapture or heights of contemplation. As Karl Rahner pointed out, the process in which human beings are created, redeemed and made holy takes place even when God is only present "anonymously" in people's lives. That is, God is ever present and active among us, but in the lives of many people that presence is largely implicit rather than explicit. Neither the word "God" nor any of the divine names might ever cross someone's lips, yet this does not mean that the Spirit is not at work in that person's life. The church confirmed this teaching at Vatican II.[3]

Similarly, the presence of the neighbor may turn out to have been really implicit in a person's relatedness to God. The solitary contemplative lost in the depths of the divine mystery might not be aware of it, but all of his or her sisters and brothers are necessarily there too. For if it is truly God that we encounter, then we are stepping at the same time into the presence of all God's people, who have arrived, we might say, "anonymously." God, and certainly the God of Jesus, never appears to us alone. Susan Griffin drew a marvelous analogy between the human psyche and the way events of nature become embedded and preserved within stones. "It is said," she writes, "that the close study of stones will reveal traces from fires suffered thousands of years ago...part of the cycle of life." And: "No detail that enters the mind, nor the smallest instance of memory, ever really leaves it, and things we had thought forgotten will arise suddenly to consciousness years later, or, undetected, shape the course of our lives."[4]

To follow the insight here, if the cells of our bodies carry traces of the history of life from millions of years ago, and if our minds carry the imprint of events from our personal and collective pasts, then as creatures we are not at our core truly solitary. We are living testimony to a profound solidarity with the earth and with other men and women which the abstract-sounding term "human nature" tends to obscure. Solidarity becomes us as much spiritually and religiously as it does physically and psychologically. The life of prayer includes both our becoming conscious of that solidarity and our embracing ever more fully the implications of the human soul's oneness with all men and women.

There is something in the passage from *Ghosts of Manila*, however, which raises a disturbing prospect. "Losing your faith is like giving up smoking," it says. "You suddenly realize that countless millions are getting by without it." Is faith so effortlessly laid aside? Is faith no different from smoking? Could humanity detach itself from faith the way we let go of outmoded scientific ideas or empty social assumptions about race and gender? Is faith nothing more than a piece of cultural clothing we might shed at will? It is true, of course, that many people do "get by" without believing that they were created by a loving God, or that Jesus Christ was raised from the dead. So what, finally, is faith all about? Is it really necessary? Someone might reply that particular beliefs within a religion may be expendable, but that faith itself is as vital a requirement for the well-being of the human spirit as proper nutrition is for our bodies. Still, if individual beliefs were to disappear, then most likely so would the disposition of faith which stands behind them.

We could, of course, quibble with the speaker in this passage. We could argue that if "wishing to live my life well" amounts to "helping others to do the same," then at least some *minimal* faith must be involved. He *believes*, does he not, that helping others is essential to his living well? He *believes* that "others" are worth helping, that there is something about them which justifies his energy and selfless activity on their behalf. His basic act of faith, therefore, must be in the dignity and value of the human person.

We could imagine someone objecting, however, that it is quite possible to live well even without this basic belief about human life as deserving of respect, attention and service. What appears to justify the speaker's faith in this case is not a philosophical appeal to God as the transcendent foundation or guarantor of the value and dignity of human beings, but an appeal to experience: "The discovery that wishing to live my life well means helping others to do the same is oddly *strengthening and calming*." Ultimately, the speaker's justification for his conviction about why he does what he does is his experience. The "discovery" makes him strong and brings him some measure of peace, perhaps even happiness. He has discovered that he can live without

God, but that he cannot be at peace without living for others. Or to state the point differently, he can survive as a human being without God, but he cannot remain human apart from solidarity with others.

Yet what sort of resolution is this? The contrast between the neighbor we do see and the God whom we do not see is not a contrast between the concrete and the abstract. God may not be immediately visible, but God is no abstraction. God becomes an abstraction, however, when the divine reality is conceived apart from God's solidarity with us, and as an abstraction God is easily dismissed. We cannot pray to an idea.

The Christian Self Is Not Solitary

In the prelude to his book *A Way in the World*, V. S. Naipaul remarked:

> Most of us know the parents or grandparents we come from. But we go back and back, forever; we go back all of us to the very beginning; in our blood and bone and brain we carry the memories of thousands of beings....We cannot understand all the traits we have inherited. Sometimes we are strangers to ourselves.[5]

The idea expressed here can shed light on the reality of faith, in the way of Susan Griffin's lesson from the "life" of stones. For not only do we relate, consciously and freely, to the holy mystery of God (which is what makes us believers); we also relate to all other human beings, both in the past and in the present. The person who has no faith—no relationship to God—in any sense of the word is a stranger to himself. So also, the one who has no sense of her fundamental relatedness to the countless thousands of human beings whom we carry inside of us has no comprehension of just who and what she is. She, too, would be a stranger to herself.

To overcome this alienation from oneself, a person needs to be able to discover that self in other people. By coming into close contact with men and women who are believers, that is, people for whom relatedness to God is both real and conscious, I might become a believer, too. And by coming into close contact with the poor and marginalized people of the world, I am apt to discover the many thousands who have left their legacies buried in our common soul. In short, believers awaken me to my relatedness to God, and the poor awaken me to my relatedness to all of God's people.

Faith, I have been arguing, consists of two conceptually distinct but concretely inseparable moments: God and the neighbor. We exist in relationship to both. Since prayer is the way we ordinarily give voice to faith, when we pray we create a space for both.

God and neighbor are not quantitifiable, as if we could measure and determine how much of God belongs in our prayer and how much of our neighbor. Whenever and wherever we allow God to be present to us, there and then we are also in the presence of our sisters and brothers. Whenever and wherever we let God's people be present to us, there and then we have stepped into the presence of God. The person who, each time he sits down to eat, tries to be mindful of those in the world who have little or nothing on their tables is placing himself in the presence of the world's poor. The person who wants to know by whose hands and under what conditions the clothes she is about to buy were made, lest she unwittingly lend support to inhumane working conditions or exploitative wages, is aligning herself with victims of oppression everywhere. The face of a starving woman recalled from the morning newspaper, the memory of unemployed men at a soup

kitchen, the long, silent, famished lines of refugees we see
on the evening news, slum children with swollen bellies:
the poor crush into our lives from many directions, and as
they come pouring in, so too does God.

The purpose of Christian prayer is not to uncover
divine solutions to the social and economic problems of
our nation or of the world. Prayer does not displace the
task of creative, intelligent and compassionate research
and discussion, civic collaboration, or political action. In
fact, prayer is never a means to an end; it is not "practical"
in the customary sense of the word. Nevertheless, prayer
remains a profound expression of who we are as men and
women; it is a sign of our having been made for one
another, and it reveals the mystery within the humanity
which all of us share. Prayer involves a continual movement back and forth between our inner space and the
world in which we live. Drawing upon the images, concerns and experiences which daily pour into us, prayer
shapes and reshapes consciousness itself.

How Helpful Is the Example of Abraham?

Within our religious tradition, perhaps no one has
come to symbolize or embody faith more than Abraham,
the first of Israel's great patriarchs. According to the biblical story, God suddenly entered Abraham's life, called him
to be the father of a great nation and promised him land
and offspring. When in his old age Abraham still had no
son, a heavenly messenger tells him that his aged wife
Sarah will conceive and indeed bear a child. Many centuries later, Paul would write:

> Hoping against hope, he believed that he would
> become "the father of many nations," according to

what was said, "So numerous shall your descendants be." (Rom 4:18)

And the letter to the Hebrews would state:

By faith Abraham obeyed when he was called to set out for a place that he was to receive as an inheritance; and he set out, not knowing where he was going. By faith he stayed for a time in the land he had been promised, as in a foreign land, living in tents, as did Isaac and Jacob, who were heirs with him of the same promise....By faith he received power of procreation, even though he was too old—and Sarah herself was barren—because he considered him faithful who had promised. Therefore from one person, and this one as good as dead, descendants were born, "as many as the stars of heaven and as the innumerable grains of sand by the seashore." (Heb 11:8–9, 11–12)

On the basis of texts like these, it would seem that faith essentially boils down to believing that God can do the impossible. The greater the odds, the stiffer the challenge, the more God appears to relish the great leap of faith men and women must take. On this showing, faith means trusting that God can do all things. As a result, Abraham's story is one that religious writers return to repeatedly in order to encourage believers whose faith might be under pressure not to abandon God. Even the evangelists appear to share such a view. Luke records the angel reassuring Mary, "For nothing will be impossible with God" (Lk 1:37), and Mark recalls an instruction of Jesus:

"Have faith in God. Truly I tell you, if you say to this mountain, 'Be taken up and thrown into the sea,' and if you do not doubt in your heart, but believe that what you say will come to pass, it will be done for you." (Mk 11:22–23)

But such an approach to faith may lead us into a worrisome spirituality. For one thing, we have to wonder what sort of God has actually been revealed to us in scripture. On the one hand, God has endowed human beings with reason, intelligence and judgment. And yet on the other hand, God seems to delight in short-circuiting reasonableness in favor of the miraculous. Moreover, God apparently does this for no other "reason" than to confound the wisdom of the wise:

> Where is the one who is wise? Where is the scribe? Where is the debater of this age? Has not God made foolish the wisdom of the world? (1 Cor 1:20)

Once again, I believe, we are running up against God as a literary character. Any presentation of faith which juxtaposes faith with reason is going to run into the sort of theological paradox we have just pointed out. Perhaps in the above text Paul had in mind that faith concerns a higher form of reasonableness.

Yet the fact of the matter is that matters of fundamental belief are usually placed in a privileged category all by themselves, to be welcomed and embraced as symbolic representations of the way things are. We may devote some time to thinking about what we believe, as when we enroll in a bible study class or listen to an engaging homily or face one of life's major crises. But ultimately the truths and symbols of our faith, we concede, exceed the power of human comprehension. And this gets us back to square one.

A second difficulty inherent in stories like that of Abraham is that God is portrayed as someone who constantly *tests* his creatures either to measure their fidelity or to force them to mature. In Abraham's case, the greatest test of all had to be the moment when God commanded him to sacrifice his son Isaac (Gen 22:2). Even Jesus is said

to have learned obedience through the things which he suffered (Heb 5:8). He was "tested," just as we are (Heb 4:15;
see also Lk 4:13). Such testing is a form of disciplining us,
"for the Lord disciplines those whom he loves" (Heb 12:6).

There is, of course, a very basic sort of testing which
takes place throughout the whole of our lives: life itself
may be said to "test" us. But testing is a metaphor. It is a
way of making sense out of our experience of being
stretched, pulled, taught, chastened, humbled, toughened,
and made wise. God does not "test" human beings by bar-
raging them with a host of problems and tragedies, like the
ones Satan visited on the unfortunate Job. When we say,
therefore, that we are being tested, or that God is testing us,
we are in effect endeavoring to make sense out of some
particularly difficult circumstances.

A third limitation of the story is that it depicts
Abraham's *physical journeying* as further confirmation of
the depth of his faith:

> Now the Lord said to Abram, "Go from your country
> and your kindred and your father's house to the land
> that I will show you." (Gen 12:1)

Thus begins the wandering of Abraham in response to
God's call, and countless men and women have uncovered
in this text the quintessential divine invitation to undertake
a journey. The confessional text which begins, "A wandering Aramean was my ancestor" (Deut 26:5), becomes a
perennial acknowledgment of the human condition itself.
To be human is to be on pilgrimage.

Yet journeying, too, is basically a metaphor which is
supposed to help us arrange and interpret our experience.
For some people journey has been a rich, fruitful image.
But in order for Abraham to take possession of the land
which God had promised him, other people would have to

be displaced. And that seems as unfair and unholy as the exploitation and destruction wrought by colonial powers when they came to the New World. Merchants, soldiers, and even some missionaries navigated to the Americas under the misguided belief that by enabling the process of evangelization they were justified in making their own the promised land of silver and gold. Needless to say, the mere fact that people worship other gods is not enough to grant justice a holiday.

We can wonder further about the adequacy of the journey metaphor itself, which is so easily spiritualized. Some people habitually use the word *journey* to describe a process of interior growth and the development of self-knowledge, but Abraham's journeying is not about growth and discovery. In the Genesis story, God *literally* called Abraham as part of a larger plan to form the people of Israel. But this encounter does not apply to the rest of us for at least three reasons.

First, we have no information as to how Abraham actually "heard" the divine voice, but if he really did hear something, then his experience of God's dealings with human beings can in no way be considered normative. Our more likely reaction is to dismiss the historical reliability of the story, since people who claim to hear divine voices today are generally considered either crazy or dangerous.

Second, we have not been singled out to be mothers and fathers of new nations. Besides, we would find it hard to envision that God was ever in the business of parceling out real estate.

Third, most of us have to learn how to love and serve God without ever setting foot outside of familiar territory. It is difficult to imagine what special interest God might have in asking people to set out on journeys, unless the divine purpose is basically spiritual, that is, motivating us to live without clutter and to realize how transitory our existence in this world is.

Although it may initially sound attractive, I do not think this last explanation really works, either. However appealing simplicity of life might be to the ascetically minded, we should not be too quick to claim that rigorous spiritual practices are what God demands of us. In the case of some individuals lean, tidy, uncluttered living may actually be a luxury, while in other cases it may be an obsession. And however sobering the fact of our transitoriness may be, it is perplexing to think of God creating the world, blessing it, endowing us with the capacity to enjoy creation both spiritually and sensually, and then reminding us that everything is passing and that we should not get attached to anything here.

In short, the story of Abraham provides us with a rather limited paradigm when it comes to analyzing faith. It also deceives us into thinking that coming to faith involves a mysterious encounter between God and the solitary individual. We need to wonder, Where are "the others" in the Abraham story? Where does the world break in?

How Helpful Is the Example of Peter?

If Abraham has come to symbolize faith, so too has the disciple Peter. The gospel story frequently cited as an example of faith is that of Peter attempting to walk on the water and nearly drowning. According to the gospel account, Jesus approached his disciples who were in a boat with the wind and the waves violently against them. The disciples are terrified, Jesus reassures them, and then Peter speaks:

"Lord, if it is you, command me to come to you on the water." He said, "Come." So Peter got out of the boat, started walking on the water, and came toward Jesus. But when he noticed the strong wind, he became frightened, and beginning to sink, he cried out, "Lord, save me!" Jesus immediately reached out his hand and caught him, saying to him, "You of little faith, why did you doubt?" (Mt 14:28–31)

If we truly believed in Jesus as the Son of God, the point seems to be, then we would not hesitate to venture the impossible. Yet once more we ask, "Is this what faith means: never doubting that, if Jesus commands us to do something, we shall not fail?" Peter's fright is understandable; it is a reaction that we recognize in ourselves whenever we become aware of "the strong wind" blowing against us in the form of challenges, suffering and unavoidable risks.

But to measure the depth of faith by one's readiness to step on the waves is hardly helpful. Indeed, we share the conviction of the gospel writer that God will not abandon us in hard moments, but we are prudent enough to realize that some steps ought not to be followed literally. One side of me relishes the story as a metaphor for situations I frequently find myself in, but experience does not permit me to think of God as the master of impossible situations.

To be fair to the evangelist, however, we have to remember that walking on the water was Peter's idea, not Jesus'. It was Peter who was trying to authenticate Jesus' presence: "Lord, if it is you…" Peter was laying down the condition for Jesus to prove it was really he, a condition not unlike the challenge Satan put down for Jesus: If you are the Son of God, prove it! (Mt 4:1–11). Peter's nearly drowning, therefore, was of his own doing.

Maybe the story is not so clearly about strength of faith after all. It may contain a veiled warning against putting the Lord to the test. Jesus' word, "Take heart, it is I; do not be afraid," ought to be enough to reassure the fearful disciples. God does not require the impossible of us; neither should we require the impossible of God.

In short, neither Abraham's story nor Peter's may be immediately helpful for understanding what faith is all about. In fact, they can even render faith a disservice, especially whenever biblical stories lead us to assume that faith means believing God can do the impossible, as if God, by definition, were not Love (as the first letter of John tells us), but the Master of impossible situations. Looked at that way, does not faith amount to the ultimate human defense against the insanity of life? Human reason defends itself against irrationality by maintaining that an ultimate power governs the universe, even if that power does not regularly respond to human needs and requests. But people who spend their lives waiting for impossible things to happen generally wind up disappointed and disillusioned.

We could, of course, turn the thought around along the lines of another gospel text: "for God all things are possible" (Mt 19:26). Maybe it would be truer to experience to think of faith as a surrender to a God who creates fresh *possibilities*. Conceived this way, faith shows its active or responsive aspect. By the time we reach the point of relying on God to accomplish the impossible, there is clearly nothing else for us to do except wait on God. But when we think of God as the one who fashions new possibilities, then at least we are opening ourselves to face boldly the circumstances of our life and times. It is up to us to take initiatives, even when the only choice left to us is to resign ourselves to the inevitable. Submission to the will of God, to draw upon a traditional spiritual theme, is essentially an active, not a passive attitude for a person of genuine faith. Doing and accepting the will of God is always a matter of sober, deliberate, open-eyed choice. And that choice is itself one of the possibilities God sets before us.

How Alone Was Abraham After All?

The Abraham story would not be helpful to a contemporary spirituality if it were to lead us to concentrate on the testing, the journeying, the blind obedience or even God's direct dealing with Abraham *as an individual*. What should not be overlooked, however, is the fact that through Abraham a new people will come into existence. Abraham, then, does not stand alone as a model for all time of a private and privileged relationship to God; he stands at the head of a nation.

To think of Abraham is to think of progeny, to be sure. But more importantly to think of Abraham is to bring to mind the entire people of Israel. At the time when the Lord spoke to him and promised to make of him a great nation, Abraham could not see that future people; only God could envision the prospect of people as numerous as the sands of the shore or the stars of the sky (Gen 22:17). Indeed, from a purely literary point of view, the very fact that so many readers have identified with various portions of the biblical narrative about Abraham should be enough to remind us that by representing the primordial person of faith Abraham in some sense has become all believers. They resonate with his story because they see their experience at least broadly patterned after his. In a similar fashion, by representing the person struggling to understand and to follow Jesus despite great personal inadequacy the figure of Peter has virtually become all disciples.

If there is a thread which unifies the great call stories in scripture, it is the fact that the divine call is always situated in terms of a mission *to the people*. In the case of Moses

God says, "I have observed the misery of my people who
are in Egypt" (Ex 3:7). The prophets, of course, are called in
order to proclaim God's word to the people of Israel, and in
the case of Jeremiah even to all the nations: "I appointed
you a prophet to the nations" (Jer 1:5). Paul had no doubt
that he had been called to proclaim the gospel to the
Gentiles (Rom 1:1, 5; Acts 9:15), while Luke glosses the
vocation of Jesus with a text from Isaiah about bringing
good news to the poor, freedom to the oppressed and liberty to captives (Lk 4:18–19). The disciples called by Jesus
are sent on mission throughout the towns and villages of
Galilee, and eventually their successors will travel even
farther. In other words, built into the very idea of call is,
from the Spirit's side, the people who matter to God.

By reading the great biblical call narratives as if the
center of attention were the individual being summoned,
even summoned to a mission, we overlook what is opera-
tive from the divine side. God's attention is always on the
people, and the one called will pour out his or her life,
sometimes figuratively and other times literally, for the
sake of other men and women. In every case, through the
ones called, whether patriarchs or prophets, apostles or
teachers, God is summoning the whole community to
renewed faith and reformed practice. Moreover, the direction of that renewal and reform is nearly always to the
advantage and the deliverance of the downtrodden, the
poor, the victims of injustice, the lowly.

If we ever think of ourselves standing before God in
the manner of an Abraham, it is frightfully important for us
to remember that God does not behold us alone, for when
the Lord looked at Abraham, he beheld the whole people
of Israel. And if we feel ourselves invited to share
Abraham's celebrated trust, then it must be a trust properly placed. We always need to beware of the individual-

ism, even the self-centeredness, which can unwittingly spring up in our interior life. Reading biblical texts we ought to be careful not to appropriate them in a way that essentially privatizes them. The solitary individual before God is not the best way to picture what the spiritual life looks like.

If faith without works is dead, as the letter of James warns us, then faith without solidarity is also dead. When a person's relationship with God turns into a private and solitary affair, the act of faith might not be all that different, say, from smoking. You can give it up and manage to live well without it. But when the act of faith inserts us into the lives of other men and women, into the history of human suffering and hope, one could no more give up one's faith in God than one could stop breathing.

3

The Election of Israel or the Adoption of the Poor?

Making sense of our lives in religious terms is something we do more or less continually. When bad things happen we may ask how God who is supposed to be goodness itself could have allowed it. Or when suffering strikes, we may find a ready answer to account for pain and tragedy in the cross of Jesus. No matter how ominous the world around us might appear, we steady our religious nerves with the conviction that everything lies in God's hands, or we remind ourselves with Paul that "all things work together for good for those who love God" (Rom 8:28). In short, we could not continue to pray without relying on some view of divine providence to account for the why and wherefore of things that happen to us.

This process of making religious sense of things can be observed in the Wisdom literature of the Old Testament and in a number of places in the New. The question the disciples posed to Jesus, "Rabbi, who sinned, this man or his parents, that he was born blind?" (Jn 9:2), was actually wrong-headed, because physical illness or disability does not signal divine punishment. But the question does illustrate an ancient effort to account for suffering in the world. The early followers of Jesus, to cite another example, found themselves having to make sense of his suffering and death. After all, why should the Son of God, of all people, have had to undergo such a humiliating death?

For their answers, the disciples and the first Christian communities turned to the scriptures and to Israel's cultic categories which were ready to hand. They were unable to tell the Jesus story without recourse to imagery drawn from the temple, priesthood, purification practices, animal sacrifice, and so forth. They explained his death in terms of sacrifice and sin offering, they believed that the events of Jesus' life had been prefigured in the scriptures, and they even composed scenes which brought together the Old and the New. The transfiguration story shows Jesus in conversation with Moses and Elijah about his approaching death, and then we hear the divine voice confirming Jesus as the beloved Son. At a stroke, continuity with the great prophetic traditions of Israel is affirmed, the tragic death of Jesus is presented as part of God's saving plan, and Jesus is revealed as God's beloved, to whom obedience should be given. All this belongs to the process of making sense of things.[1]

Interpreting the life and death of Jesus in terms of the scriptures also shows us the important role played by the biblical texts themselves in people's lives, while its recourse to Israel's worship and ritual positioned the Christian community to develop its own distinctive adaptation of Jewish liturgy. The community's liturgical life, in turn, would figure significantly in how believers continually discover fresh meaningfulness in their lives. They would join themselves inwardly to the mystery of the Christ who dies and rises symbolically or sacramentally. Paul demonstrates this when he reminds the Roman Christians about the meaning of their baptism:

> Therefore we have been buried with him by baptism into death, so that, just as Christ was raised from the

> dead by the glory of the Father, so we too might walk
> in newness of life. (Rom 6:4)

And he instructs the Corinthian Christians in a similar way about the meaning of the eucharist:

> For as often as you eat this bread and drink the cup,
> you proclaim the Lord's death [both in the liturgy and
> in daily life] until he comes. (1 Cor 11:26)

Yet the biblical writings in particular provided a reservoir of meaning from which Christians could draw freely as they attempted to make sense of their lives and even the whole of history.

But perhaps there is no place in the New Testament where the attempt to interpret history and one's experience is so sustained and gripping as in chapters nine, ten and eleven of Paul's letter to the Romans. There Paul is thinking his way through the theological significance of the rejection of the gospel by Israel as a whole (some Jews obviously had embraced it) and the new status of the Gentiles in God's plan of salvation. In the end, Paul's resolution of these issues may not be all that satisfying, but what he was attempting contains an important lesson for us.

The Difficulty with the Notion of Election

Paul's problem appears to arise from his belief that the people of Israel were God's chosen or elected ones, and God's decision to choose, indeed to adopt Israel as a father would adopt a child, was sealed with a promise or covenant.[2] Being ever faithful, the Lord could never go back on his word. Now Israel as a whole has rejected the gospel, something Paul finds immensely difficult to fathom. He hits upon a way of dealing with that rejection by reasoning along the following lines. The rejection of the gospel by the Jews has forced a mission to the Gentiles, and therefore it turns out that Jewish hardness of heart is providential. Nevertheless, Paul cannot accept the prospect that Israel's rejection of what God has done in Christ will be permanent. Eventually, Israel will be saved. Paul writes:

> ...I want you to understand this mystery: a hardening has come upon part of Israel, until the full number of the Gentiles has come in. And so all Israel will be saved....As regards the gospel they [the people of Israel] are enemies of God for your sake; but as regards election they are beloved, for the sake of their ancestors. (Rom 11:25–26, 28)

In the course of his reasoning, Paul operates with at least three assumptions. First, drawing on several key texts from the Hebrew scriptures, Paul believes that God, for reasons hidden within the divine mystery, had chosen or elected Israel. God "has mercy on whomever he chooses, and he hardens the heart of whomever he chooses" (9:18). In the Exodus story, for example, God hardened the Pharaoh's heart; according to the story in Genesis 27 about Isaac's two sons, God loved Jacob but "hated" Esau (that is, God loved Esau less). Yet scripture also gave Paul the support he needed to defend God's determination to include Gentiles among his people. The idea of a God who elects and chooses had created Paul's theological problem, which he solved by appealing to the sovereignty of God. Paul accepts that this is what God is like. And although he has no inkling as to how or when it will come about, Paul does not doubt that one day Israel too will find its salvation.

The second assumption Paul made, then, was that so long as Israel refused the gospel ("persisting in unbelief") it had temporarily forfeited the divine favor. He also warns his Gentile readers that the faith of Israel is their "root," and that if they themselves fall into unbelief they too will be cut off from the promise. Paul may have been convinced that those Jews who had rejected his preaching and remained faithful to their Judaism could not be pleasing to God. But what about those Jews whose faith was genuine, who understood very well that salvation depended upon more than sheer observance of the law? What about those who were devout yet still did not feel compelled to follow Christ, because they did not believe him to be the Messiah of Israel? Paul's theology does not seem to allow for this possibility.

The third assumption from which Paul operated was that there had to be consistency in God. By that I mean something all of us would probably assent to in some form or other, namely, a continuity between the "old" and the "new." The coming of Christ could never signal a complete rupture within God's saving action in human history. The idea of divine fidelity prohibits one from thinking that God might break a promise or decide to abandon Israel altogether. The God of Israel was still the God of Jesus and the God of the Christians. Thus there must be a continuity of divine aims as we move from the biblical account of creation, the stories of the patriarchs, the events of Exodus, the time of the judges and prophets, and so forth, into the days of John the Baptist, the ministry of Jesus, the sending of the Spirit and the work of the apostles.[3]

Yet God, not as the holy, silent mystery but as the literary character, is not altogether consistent in scripture; God is *rendered* consistent as a result of theological reflection like that of Paul and the evangelists. The problem Paul is attempting to resolve, in other words, is not actually a problem with the mystery of God in itself; it is a difficulty with God as a literary character and historical actor. Paul was dealing with the revered, ancient texts in which his intellect and imagination were steeped. But they were still human texts and they "suffered" from all the limitations of human composition.

It could be argued, therefore, that God as the unfathomable mystery does not elect and adopt one nation over others, or one group, or one social class, or one religious community, or one individual over all others *for absolutely no reason.* It could be argued further that the majority of the Jewish people could have decided not to follow Jesus and still have been justified (to use Paul's term) on the basis of their faith. Paul might not have been able to grant that, given the dynamics of his own religious transformation, but we certainly can.

And finally, it could be argued that the need for consistency speaks more about us than about God. For not only is the literary character of God problematic at a number of points throughout the bible, but no individual's (or community's) experience of God is so exhaustive as to be the universal religious experience. Israel's experience of God was not exempt from the perspectivism which affects all of us. This means that God could have continued to reach the Jewish people in and through their traditions, beliefs and practices, and still initiate a new and distinctive relationship with the Gentiles. In fact, Paul himself pries open this possibility by his insistence upon the priority of faith over works. If we take "works" to include not just all our moral actions but our religious observance and the liturgical and doctrinal forms which express our faith as well, then being related to God by faith becomes the foundation of every authentic expression of human religiosity.

There is a deeper difficulty here, however, perhaps brought on by the absence of Jesus stories in Paul's correspondence to anchor the imagination and to provide it with some outer limits. While it is no doubt true that the evangelists were not writing exactly as historians, the literary form they chose to employ combined traditions, memories and sayings in a way that conferred upon them the semblance of being a history. The effect of this literary form was that it forever rooted Christian thinking and imagination within history, even though many of the elements of the gospel narrative are not historical in our sense of the word.

Paul, on the other hand, seems to prescind from history. His Jesus, who is actually the risen Christ of the church's faith, now reigns gloriously with the Father. But there is no readily discernible insistence in Paul that this Jesus at one time also ate and drank among us, and interacted with all kinds of people. His earthly life becomes strangely uninteresting, overshadowed by the grand mystery of the cross and resurrection. Yet that earthly existence is profoundly important to us for our estimation of everyday life. While our final dwelling place may lie in heaven, we would not want to parachute out of this life prematurely. Even in the face of grave violence and injustice, and widespread human suffering, we would first choose a transformed earth to a speedy exit to everlasting life. Such a preference, in fact, is far more in keeping with Jesus' own hope in the kingdom of God as a possibility for this world.

This complaint against Paul may be unfair. Paul wrote letters, not a gospel, and we have no idea just how much more he knew about Jesus which he either presupposed his readers were familiar with or which he shared with them in person. Nevertheless, the impression left by the correspondence makes one abundantly grateful for the evangelists. For even Paul's most eloquent writing on the mystery of Christ has an odd, ahistorical ring to it. The rhythm of dying and rising can be heard or perceived in many aspects of our lives; it is hardly an exclusively Christian theme. Nature itself acts out dying and rising in the annual passage of seasons. What dying and rising mean in a Christian context needs to be pitched against the actual reasons for Jesus' arrest and crucifixion. He was not arrested and sentenced to die in order to facilitate a divine plan for reconciling God and the world. Yet for Paul those actual, historical reasons do not emerge as critical to his grasp of Jesus' death. The theological significance of that death thereby carries greater weight than the history leading up to the cross. Indeed, the Christian faith includes both historical and symbolic dimensions, and to stress either of these at the expense of the other introduces a note of unreality into our prayer.

But our concern is not with the whole of Paul's thinking about Jesus. Rather, we are interested in the question he is working his way through regarding Israel's rejection of the promise (as represented by Christ) and the subsequent offer of salvation to the Gentiles. The promise of salvation (we might also say the promise which is salvation) has been transferred to a new people. One has only to read Romans 9–11 to review how Paul comes to terms with this transfer. He knows firsthand that the Gentiles have been given the Spirit, and he also believes that Israel's refusal to accept the gospel gave God no choice but to cut away the fruitless branches. Still, he holds with all his heart that permanent infidelity cannot be the case. There will be a conversion on the part of the Jewish nation. It is almost like saying that the wicked tenants who were dislodged from the vineyard will one day recognize the error of their ways and repent, considering how long-suffering the owner had been (see Mt 21:33–41).

God Elects the Poor

Maybe Paul's wrestling and reasoning have to be shifted into a different key. Let us suppose that the promise of God or salvation has *always* been intended for everyone, since God is not first of all Israel's God but the God of all nations, however potentially troublesome this idea might be.[4] In other words, perhaps *all nations have been elected*, or specially chosen and loved. Let us suppose further that salvation has two aspects: salvation from death in the traditional sense of the gift of everlasting life, and salvation from the historical forms of sin, alienation and death which afflict human beings and their societies here and now, such as poverty, ignorance and political or social oppression.[5] And let us suppose, finally, that the message about salvation has been entrusted to a community of faith or to "a people that produces the fruits of the kingdom," as the parable of the vineyard puts it (Mt 21:43).

What then would happen if this new people proved to be faithless with the message they had been given? What if they no longer produced "fruits of the kingdom"? What if the promise of salvation should be aborted while in their care? What in other words would happen if the church of God, that new people, failed in its charge? Then, we could imagine, God would choose another to be the bearer of the promise. Paul would probably have found that prospect as unpalatable as the evangelist Matthew would have.

That impasse leads us to envision a different possibility. Turning faithless and thus meriting rejection occur when people no longer live out of and for the divine promise. We fail when we no longer trust in the power of the Spirit to bring about the kingdom of God. And the critical factor causing many of us to forget that promise and become complacent about the way things are is our loss of contact with men and women who have not experienced divine salvation in any form. In short, the defining mark of faithlessness, from a Christian point of view, is losing one's solidarity with the poor and oppressed. Having lost that, there is absolutely no reason for hope, for nobody hopes for what he already has.

To state this idea positively, the attitude of faith which makes us righteous before God is our oneness with the masses of the world's poor in their aspiring and striving for that "new heaven and new earth" (Rev 21:1) which God presents to them in and through the story of Jesus. They are the chosen ones, and the rest of us will have to find our place among God's people in a union of minds and hearts with them. God rejects and turns away empty those who have never hungered and thirsted for righteousness. God prunes away the fruitless branches: the ones who think that piety alone, or worship alone, or never breaking the law, will be enough to win divine mercy and favor. Paul gave us an important lesson in that regard: "For we hold that a person is justified by faith apart from works prescribed by the law" (Rom 3:28).

What Paul did not consider, however, was another way of conceiving membership in God's people. Paul realized that being numbered among the chosen ones had nothing to do with ethnicity and physical descent, because he wrote:

> This means that it is not the children of the flesh who are the children of God, but the children of the promise are counted as descendants. (Rom 9:8)

More to the point, he also understood that it had nothing to do with personal merit, as if one could lay title to grace because of his or her own effort. Joseph Fitzmyer comments:

> If the olive tree stands for the group of those who believe in Christ, the "root" of which is Adam, who, though called as a pagan, became the person of faith,

there is then no sole ethnic ground for membership. Gentile Christians and the remnant are all God's people united in the same faith; they are "Israel" in the eschatological sense. True, Paul has already accorded Israel in the ethnic sense a priority because of its historical call (1:16; 2:9–10); chronologically it has precedence over the Gentiles in God's plan. The pagan Abraham was first called by God to become the "root" of the Jewish people, and to them Jesus first announced his gospel. Thus the Jewish patriarch is the "root" of the church, Jewish and Gentile. Once again Paul singles out the Jewish people because of their historic role as the first children of Abraham and is concerned that Gentile Christians do not lose sight of their connections and their roots.[6]

Yet what Paul is getting at in his letter could never be clearer than in the case of the world's poor, for their condition has nothing to do with anything they have done or failed to do. Those who boast that they escaped poverty and ignorance by dint of personal effort and hard work deceive themselves if they think that this is what makes them righteous in God's eyes.

The world's poor are the people of God. The basis of their election or adoption is not ethnicity, but social condition. Poverty is their father, not Abraham. There is no escaping their world, even if by accident of birth we do not share the burdens of poverty, violence and injustice, or even if we are among those who managed to work their way out of the wretchedness that so many people endure. Theirs is the world we have to carry in our hearts if we want to walk blameless before God.

There may have been no reason imaginable for God to choose Jacob over his brother Esau, but there is surely a reason for God, whom the tradition calls a *saving* God, to choose the world's voiceless poor over those in the world who enjoy great prosperity, power and comfort. It might be pity, or compassion, or even outrage over their condition, but there is a logic to the divine preference. Perhaps it must be along just such lines that the real distinction between God the literary character and God the holy mystery is finally revealed. The God of the bible is certainly a literary character and historical actor, but the story of God does not start with the writing of biblical texts. God's story begins in human history, in the lives and experience of men and women. Our sacred texts presuppose the mystery of God; they do not create it.

4

To Hear God's Word, Face the World

Effective story tellers manage to draw their listeners and readers into their narration not only by the cadence and elegance of their language, but also by enabling their audience to perceive a connection between the story they are being told and their own lives. Any adult who has caught a youngster's attention with a story has learned this lesson. The child's imagination takes over the story and the child becomes a participant in the narrative adventure.

The evangelists certainly were effective narrators of the story of Jesus, for his story has survived to intrigue and inspire countless generations over nearly twenty centuries. The genius of the gospel accounts, of course, is to be found not only in each evangelist's technique as a writer, but also in the strong faith which has been bequeathed to us by preachers, family members, teachers and catechists and worshiping communities, Christian artists and poets and musicians, and saints and theologians. Without that living faith—that "cloud of witnesses" (Heb 12:1)—the gospels would amount to little more than quaint religious texts, full of interesting but untried recipes.

The greatest story of all, of course, is the story of God, of which the gospels and indeed the entire bible are only partial testimony. For the great story of God is really the

74

story of humanity in search of salvation. Whoever would tell God's story, therefore, needs more than a strong voice and graceful tongue. The story teller must be able to narrate God's story in a way that enables the listener to connect his or her life with the history of God. A contemporary gospel writer would, in fact, have to relate the world's story in such a way that every reader recognizes how he or she has been a part of that story all along, and how the principal actor in the world's story is the God who would make people whole. Jesus achieved this for the people of his day by telling parables.

At the outset of his book *The World of Jesus*, John Riches observed:

> However much some prophetic figures transcend their time, they do so precisely as men and women of their time. Standing at the doorway into a new world, they nonetheless share their contemporaries' hopes and fears and seek to lead their people out into what is to come. Their words speak to their contemporaries' condition: They may meet with opposition and incomprehension, but they also address their people's deepest hopes and desires. In their preaching and their deeds they seek to transform people's understanding of themselves and their world and prepare them to embrace the world to come. It is in this interaction with traditional, inherited beliefs and practices that they are able to exercise their extraordinary power over their contemporaries. And it is in this that their power to create new worlds resides.[1]

Riches is making the point that prophetic individuals naturally address themselves to the specific social and cultural, religious and political circumstances of their time. Or to put the observation another way, prophets might declare, "Thus says the Lord," but they must always face the world in order to know what exactly the Lord wants them to say. Riches is also pointing out that prophetic figures are in large measure created by their times. The figure of Moses, for example, is forever associated with the Pharaoh and the Jewish plight for which Egypt was responsible, while the figure of John the Baptist cannot be divorced from the Herod who had him beheaded and whose gruesome regime John had criticized. Desperate times call forth prophetic spirits.

The integrity of our prayer, we have been suggesting, depends upon two things, our solidarity with the world and our oneness with God. The Protestant theologian Karl Barth once remarked that Christians ought to make their way in the world with the bible in one hand and the daily newspaper in the other. The scriptural texts, he was suggesting, need to be read and interpreted in light of contemporary life, while the events and circumstances of the present fall under the biblical word of God for their proper illumination. Revelation happens, we might say, in the moment when scripture and the world come together in the mind and heart of a person of faith.

The faith/world dynamic which lies at the heart of Christian prayer was also at work from the very beginning, when the first Christian communities began narrating the Jesus story. The gospel was not written to meet the moral and spiritual needs of the men and women who were Jesus' contemporaries but to speak to people of a generation or two later. The primary concern of the evangelists was to enable succeeding generations to find real, everyday meaningfulness within the mystery of Christ risen, not to preserve an historically exact record of the ministry of Jesus. In order to accomplish this, the New Testament authors were understandably viewing *the present* in light of their faith in what God *had done* in and through Jesus. The present thus became the main determinant in how the story got told. It was not always evident, however, what exactly Jesus was all about, and this occasionally caused problems.

Which Jesus?

There is a fascinating collection of ancient writings which contain several accounts of Jesus' early life called "infancy gospels." The church for sound reasons excluded them from the New Testament. The following passage from the Infancy Gospel of Thomas helps us to understand why:

> When he was six years old, his mother gave him a pitcher and sent him to draw water and bring it to the house. But in the crowd he stumbled, and the pitcher was broken. But Jesus spread out the garment he was wearing, filled it with water and brought it to his mother. And when his mother saw the miracle, she kissed him, and kept to herself the mysteries which she had seen him do.[2]

The fact that the apocryphal infancy stories were able to portray the young Jesus in this manner reveals something about the implications which at least some Christians had drawn from the church's statements about him. Whoever composed the above passage apparently saw no inconsistency between the young Jesus who worked such fabulous miracles and whatever he or she had been taught about what it meant to be Son of God. To take another story:

> And after some days, as Jesus was going through the middle of the city, a certain child threw a stone at him and hit him on the shoulder. And Jesus said to him, "You shall not go on your way." And straightaway he too fell down and died. And those who happened to be there were astonished saying, "Where does this

young child come from that every word that he says
has immediate effect?" They too went and com-
plained to Joseph, saying, "You will not be able to do
well with us in this city. But if you please, teach your
child to bless and not to curse; for he slays our children and every word that he says has immediate
effect."[3]

We could assemble further examples, yet the bottom
line is that the wider church chose not to admit such writings into its official scriptures. Being divine could not have
meant Jesus' being a kitchen savior for Mary, or a holy ter-
ror around the neighborhood by causing the death of dis-
agreeable playmates!

The church did acknowledge, however, the soundness of the faith contained in passages like this one from
the letter to the Colossians:

> He is the image of the invisible God, the firstborn of
> all creation; for in him all things in heaven and on
> earth were created, things visible and invisible,
> whether thrones or dominions or rulers or powers—
> all things have been created through him and for him.
> (Col 1:15–16)

This text clearly refers to the risen Christ; it would not have
been an apt characterization of Jesus of Nazareth during
his lifetime. The church carefully differentiated the character of the earthly Jesus from that of the heavenly Christ. Yet
would it not be only logical to conclude that what Jesus
was *after* the resurrection he must also have been somehow
before? Why is it so unthinkable that the child Jesus might
have worked fairy-tale wonders? Indeed, the Christ of
Colossians comes awfully close to being a cosmically pro-
portioned symbol disguised as a human person, and thus
just as unreal as the Jesus of the infancy gospels.

Where then do we find the "real Jesus" against whom we measure the pictures of Jesus that we carry in our imaginations? Why do we accept an image that says yes to miracles during Jesus' ministry but no to miracles in his childhood, or that says yes to Colossians but no to the Infancy Gospel of Thomas? What is the norm which governs the boundaries of belief, the parameters of orthodoxy?

To reply that we find Jesus in the four official or "canonical" gospels would beg the question. Even the four gospels contain some legendary elements as well as a considerable amount of interpretation, as we shall see in a moment. The nineteenth-century German philosopher Friedrich Nietzsche observed: "There is nothing absolutely primary to be interpreted, since fundamentally everything is already interpretation."[4] Nietzsche's position would rule out any possibility of discovering a "real Jesus," since our documents provide us with a Jesus who has been transformed by the living faith of the ancient communities, not a static record of his sayings and deeds.

But we are also limited in another way as we try to locate Jesus. Henry James once wrote to a woman who had just published a historical novel:

> The "historic" novel is...condemned even in cases of labour as delicate as yours, to a fatal *cheapness*, for the simple reason that the difficulty of the job is inordinate....You may multiply the little facts that can be got from pictures and documents, relics and prints as much as you like—*the* real thing is almost impossible to do, and in its essence the whole effect is nought: I mean the invention, the representation of the old *consciousness*, the soul, the sense, the horizon, the vision of individuals in whose minds half the things that make ours, that make the modern world were non-existent. You have to *think* with your modern

apparatus as a man, a woman—or rather fifty—
whose own thinking was intensely otherwise condi-
tioned, you have to simplify back by an amazing *tour
de force*—and even then it's all humbug.[5]

In light of this passage we have to wonder what exactly
goes on when through our imaginations we insert ourselves
into the scenes of the gospel texts. James was not talking
about the gospels, of course. He was not saying, exactly, that
the "real Jesus" is inaccessible because Jesus is locked somewhere in the past. James' point is that the limitation is really
ours. We are locked in the present, no matter how much we
try to understand and recreate the past. The Jesus of our
imaginations, not unlike the Jesus of the apocryphal infancy
stories, is a product of devout reconstruction.

The merits of James' observation about the writing of
historical novels aside, the fact remains that the Christian
who wants to find Jesus in order to pray with and in him
often runs into difficulties with the New Testament texts
themselves. Those venerable texts are already interpreta-
tions, inspired by faith, from another time and place. As a
result, locating Jesus is not so straightforward as one might
wish. Not that we are prevented from praying to God (we
can always do that), but whatever image of Jesus we come
up with has to keep us firmly rooted in history and in
the present world, and not distract us with premature
thoughts of glory, a longing for supernatural occurrences,
or flights of pious fancy.

As far as I can see, what controls the limits of orthodox
images of Jesus is not some elusive norm or yardstick
within the scriptural texts themselves but something outside the bible altogether. The outside determinant is the
world; or to be more precise, it is the historical experience of
believing communities and in particular the experience of
communities of suffering. The reason is that central to every

image of Jesus is some sense of what we want God to save us from. To think of Jesus apart from God's saving action in the world is to cut him away from life. Communities of suffering know quite clearly what they want from God, and knowing what they want from God determines how they image Jesus and how they pray. For example, if these communities want to escape their present situation, then Jesus becomes the model of patient suffering and the door leading to eternal blessedness. If they want to change oppressive social and economic conditions, convinced that poverty and injustice are not God's will for them, then Jesus might become the prophetic word through whom God confronts evil and overturns the powers of the present age.

The Jesus in and through whom we speak to God is real only when he is connected to the world of men and women, and Jesus will not be connected to that world if those who pray are not related to it first. Generic needs such as deliverance from spiritual ignorance or moral paralysis, or simply the need for wise guidance, are probably not sharp enough when it comes to imaging Jesus. Universal needs like these might well support his being pictured as a teacher, an exemplar of virtue, a physician or a good shepherd, and such images may be consoling. But to be historically effective, they need to be radicalized by the cross. And why would we be led to radicalize our image of Jesus, unless we were related in some way to the experience of suffering humanity?

Throughout the ages, the lives and fortunes of the poor have been the preferred place out of which God chooses to be known. Although we speak about salvation "from sin," it is the sub-human, violent conditions that oppress and destroy people which define for us what sin is all about in the first place. As a result, we can say that fundamental to every way we conceive of salvation is the liberation of human beings and their communities from political, economic and social oppression. Such oppression *is* sin. Heaven is not the automatic divine answer to such evil, but a transformed world, the kingdom of God, is.

Maybe the answer to why the ancient church said yes to miracles during the ministry of Jesus but no to fantastic deeds during his childhood was that it realized that miracles were by definition signs of the kingdom. In the case of Jesus, miracles pointed to the reign of God. They were signs of the liberation from every form of oppression which God wanted for the world, and they confirmed the presence of the Spirit in the teaching of Jesus. Amazing feats which were in any sense self-serving or detached from Jesus' proclaiming the reign of God would have to be classified as magic. Miracles made best sense when looked at in terms of the historical experience of the people to whom Jesus was announcing the good news. The miracles, in other words, pointed toward history and wholeness, not toward the secret identity of Jesus.

The Problem of "Locating" Jesus

I have no intention of pursuing here the possible limits or boundaries to orthodox belief about Jesus. Obviously, the early church realized very well that the figure of Jesus remembered was not so plastic that it could tolerate any shape whatsoever. In using the phrase "locating Jesus," I want merely to underline the fact that the New Testament portraits of Jesus emerged as the gospel writers in particular contemplated the world around them and listened to its needs. Indeed, this is exactly what had happened to Jesus himself. The ministry and message of Jesus, and even his very person, took shape against the background of the various political, social, cultural and religious moments and conditions which defined life in Galilee in the first half of the first century. Jesus was in large measure created by his time, and it was as a first-century Jewish prophet that he would leave an indelible imprint on the subsequent course of human history.

It might be worth reviewing for a moment how extensive the reshaping of the figure of Jesus has been. Unfortunately, there does not appear to be a great amount of information that can be known with certainty about the actual figure Jesus of Nazareth. Yet what becomes increasingly evident on the basis of what we do know is that the church's constant retelling of the Jesus story, if it is to be effective, must always keep one eye fixed firmly on the world. As we already noted, in some sense the world "created" Jesus, even as the world of our day largely creates and defines who and what we are. The particular needs of the men and women of Jesus' day called forth and shaped the prophetic spirit which burned in his soul. The world, in other words, was the school for his spirit. The world taught him what to think and pray about, what to desire and work for, what to distrust and confront, what to commit himself to and what was worth dying for.

1. *Making sense of hard sayings*. Some gospel texts can be particularly ticklish to interpret and apply. What are we to do, for example, with the passage where Jesus directs a man who would first bury his father to let the dead bury their own:

> To another he said, "Follow me." But he said, "Lord, first let me go and bury my father." But Jesus said to him, "Let the dead bury their own dead; but as for you, go and proclaim the kingdom of God" (Lk 9:59–60)?

Or with the passage that whoever loves a family member more than Jesus is not worthy of him:

"Whoever loves father or mother more than me is not worthy of me; and whoever loves son or daughter more than me is not worthy of me" (Mt 10:37)?

Or with the instruction Jesus gives the rich man about selling all his possessions and donating the proceeds to the poor:

Jesus, looking at him, loved him and said, "You lack one thing; go, sell what you own, and give the money to the poor, and you will have treasure in heaven; then come, follow me" (Mk 10:21)?

Or the "perfection" texts from the sermon on the mount about not judging, not swearing, not refusing to lend, not seeking revenge, and about forgiving—even loving—one's enemies? For example:

"But I say to you, Love your enemies and pray for those who persecute you, so that you may be children of your Father in heaven; for he makes his sun rise on the evil and on the good, and sends rain on the righteous and on the unrighteous" (Mt 5:44–45; see also Mt 5:21–42).

Many gospel passages need to be contextualized if readers are not going to dismiss them as irrelevant to their living. As a matter of fact, because of the troublesome and demanding nature of certain texts, readers over the centuries have done precisely that; they contextualized. Some passages, they concluded, applied to a *special* following of Christ; those texts became the foundation for monastic and religious observance. For example, Jesus' admonition to the rich man became the basis for the vow of poverty, while the saying about being eunuchs for the kingdom of God (Mt 19:12) was pressed into service for the vow of celibacy.

In the case of Jesus' prohibition against divorce, we know that Paul believed himself empowered to overturn Jesus' express instruction (see 1 Cor 7:12–16). And in the case of the pacifism which seems to be present in a number of Jesus' sayings, the new *Catechism* has determined that non-violence could never be universally legislated. Indeed, national defense remains a moral obligation of public authorities.[6]

The net effect of all such efforts to help readers deal with hard sayings in the gospels might be exactly the opposite of what Jesus intended. We run the danger of neutralizing the gospel's unyielding message about the reign of God wherever the gospel's requirements seem unrealistic, impractical or unworkable for the vast majority of believers. Jesus, we reassure ourselves, could never have realistically expected that weak, sinful men and women with work to do and families to raise would take his words with life-and-death urgency. If we were pretty certain that the world was going to end next week, or even by the end of the year, then perhaps we would take his message with greater seriousness. But Jesus was plainly uninformed about the timing of the world's end (see Mk 13:32). Indeed, Jesus might have been less insistent in his demands if he had been able to foresee how far into the future his message would be carried.[7]

Adapting the sayings and teachings of Jesus, however, is something which even the evangelists themselves engaged in with some frequency. The gospel writers had to address the particular needs of the communities for which they wrote. For instance, when it seemed advisable to adopt the practice of fasting, someone may have created a saying of Jesus to justify its adoption, since historically it appeared that Jesus and his followers did not fast (Mk 2:18–20). And in a matter of greater moment, the evangelists felt at liberty to stress the place of the cross in Christian life when a community needed to be encouraged to embrace and persevere in suffering and persecution, as Mark did. Indeed, all human suffering apparently could be subsumed under the spiritual rubric of taking up one's cross and following Jesus every day, as Luke says:

> Then he said to them all, "If any want to become my followers, let them deny themselves and take up their cross daily and follow me." (Lk 9:23)

The fact that Jesus could never actually have said those words was beside the point. Jesus would not have been speaking about the cross as a symbol of faithful discipleship prior to his own crucifixion. The early church needed some time to transform the cross as a sign of humiliation and defeat into a symbol of life, victory and fidelity to God's cause. The transformation of the cross' significance could only have occurred in light of the resurrection.

In his extensive commentary on the passion narratives, Raymond Brown details numerous instances where the evangelists undertook editorial creativity. He points out, for example, that the reason why Luke modified the Marcan passion narrative, which Luke was following as he composed his own passion story, and depicted Jesus kneeling in the garden rather than prostrate on the ground is that Luke wanted to instruct his community on the proper posture for praying. Luke's pastoral reason evidently had nothing to do with what Jesus historically had done.[8]

2. *Paul.* In addition, Paul's appropriation of the gospel message was inevitably shaped by his background as a devout, zealous Jew and a member of the party of the Pharisees. Given Paul's conviction that he had been especially chosen by the risen Christ to be the apostle for the Gentiles, we can understand his desire not to impose on

the Gentiles any more religious obligations than were absolutely necessary (see Acts 15:10).

But the scope of Paul's theological reflection on the nature of the law and its relationship to the gospel cannot be accounted for solely on the basis of his developing missionary strategy. The great Pauline emphasis on the freedom won for us by Christ and his particular slant on the meaning of Jesus' dying and rising represent yet another shaping of the gospel message. This time, however, the shaping was done in light of *Paul's* experience and background, together with the needs and backgrounds of the largely Gentile communities for which he wrote. According to one study of Paul:

> The rural world of Galilean villages, as reflected in Jesus' parables, may have had little or no meaning in urban Christianity. Here, conversely, the image of competition in the gymnasiums (1 Cor. 9:24–27) may have attracted much more attention but again may have been foreign to the Jesus tradition. Was there a need in Corinth to deal with Pharisaism in the sense of Matthew 23? Can we imagine that in Thessalonica Jesus' violations of the Sabbath were of current concern? Yet this means that everywhere theological as well as nontheological factors must have contributed to the knowledge of Jesus being written or repressed.

And again:

> Immediately conspicuous in this characterization of the earthly One [according to Paul] is the extreme concentration on the basic meaning of Jesus' life. Gone are the villages of Galilee, the Lake of Gennesaret, and Jerusalem, including temple and priesthood. Jesus does not speak as a teacher, nor does he accomplish individual deeds. He is not baptized by John and calls

no disciples into discipleship. There are no syna-
gogues and no Passover, no Pharisees and no oppo-
nents, neither a Herod nor a Pilate. Jesus has no
"biography" and does not belong in a particular
Palestinian environment. We see only God's soteriological plan for him, his appearance "when the time
had fully come" (Gal. 4:4), the basic structure of Jesus'
life as a life for people, the burdening of the unbur-
dened and the unburdening of the burdened, and the
present Lordship of Jesus the Christ. The Pauline
churches are not supposed to memorize and actualize
Jesus' sayings but practice being crucified with him.
That alone is sufficient for salvation, because that is
enough to validate the fact that Jesus' history is an
event of God's love (Rom. 5:5–6). Therefore this alone
is the content of the gospel.[9]

One conclusion that we would have to draw from the
New Testament writings themselves is that early communities were constantly refashioning the gospel message so
that "Jesus" would be able speak to the needs and circumstances of a later time.

In its attempt to give us a clearer picture of what Jesus
and his times were actually like, biblical scholarship today
presents us with a variety of perspectives on Jesus, each of
which enjoys some basis in the New Testament texts. Jesus
was principally a healer and an exorcist,[10] a teacher along
the lines of the roving purveyors of wisdom in the ancient
world,[11] a prophet on behalf of justice and liberation from
oppression,[12] or a Spirit-filled prophet of the end time
announcing God's imminent and final judgment upon the
world,[13] and God's viceroy.[14] According to one scholar:

[Jesus'] own self-understanding did not include
thinking and speaking of himself as the Son of God
whose historical intention or purpose was to die for

the sins of the world, and his message was not about believing in him. Rather, he was a spirit person, subversive sage, social prophet, and movement founder who invited his followers and hearers into a transforming relationship with the same Spirit he himself knew, and into a community whose social vision was shaped by the core value of compassion.[15]

In short, there are many portraits of Jesus which could be assembled on the basis of the New Testament writings themselves.

One morning I asked a group of clergy whether they ever preached about Jesus himself, and if so, what model or view of Jesus they tended to rely on most. One priest answered that in his preaching he frequently portrayed Jesus as a teacher and devoted a great deal of time to explaining the content of Jesus' instruction. He probably did so, the priest explained, because he himself had spent many years in teaching adolescents. Another said that in his sermons he drew on Jesus as a model and example of faith and of right living, while a third said that his favorite image was Jesus at prayer and that he frequently preached about the interior life.

The fact that there was no shared image of Jesus which guided our preaching was somewhat surprising. The priests certainly on occasion mentioned in their preaching that Jesus was Son of God, but when I inquired under what circumstances they were likely to incorporate this belief into a homily, it became clear that the motive nearly always had to do with helping people apply the meaning of salvation to their own lives. For example, because Jesus was divine, and joined himself to our humanity, all of us have the potential of living like children of God; and from time to time everyone needs to hear this reassuring message again. We need to be reminded of our capacity for goodness and holiness. Jesus' being divine has no relevance to us unless we add the words "for us and for our salvation."

But does this realization that each of us gravitates towards his or her own idea of Jesus not leave us wondering whether the *only* thing which determines our view of Jesus is one's individual experience? Does the world around us have little or nothing to contribute to the way that we set about imaging and presenting Jesus, or do the gospels merely invite us to a spiritual free-for-all? For, like sensitive preachers, the gospel writers set many images and titles of Jesus before us without telling us that one is more appropriate than the others.

If we insist upon discovering what Jesus was actually like and what precisely he taught and stood for, we are almost certainly going to wind up frustrated at the lack of firm, definitive answers. Some early Christian communities were very ascetical; but was Jesus? Some were like charismatic prayer groups; but would Jesus have fit easily into one of those, speaking in tongues and chanting hymns? Some communities were close-knit groups fervently awaiting the second coming of Jesus and the end of the world; would Jesus have been at home among one of those? Paul encouraged the Christians at Rome to obey the civil authorities and to pay taxes; would Jesus have been at ease with that sort of advice?

Perhaps we shall in time uncover enough about the life and times of Jesus to answer these and similar questions. But even then our work will not be finished, for we must still deal with the overarching question of Jesus against the background of Jewish faith and history. If God is not capricious, then there surely must be continuity between God's aims among the people of Israel and the divine intention with respect to all the nations of the world in and through the Jesus story. Jesus does not mark a break with the past in the sense of the demise of the God of Israel. The "new covenant" which is mentioned at the Last Supper could never have meant that God had given up on Israel and had unilaterally canceled the divine promise God had made to the patriarchs, as Paul argued in the strongest possible terms:

> I ask, then, has God rejected his people? By no means!
> I myself am an Israelite, a descendant of Abraham, a member of the tribe of Benjamin. God has not rejected his people whom he foreknew…for the gifts and the calling of God are irrevocable. (Rom 11:1–2, 29)

All this means that Christian theology today has a great task ahead.[16] Our spirituality and our prayer cannot but be affected by the way we conceive salvation and the action of God in human history.

For now, the only claim I want to make is that the world plays a necessary role in the way we picture Jesus today; it always has. There is a wonderful insight behind Karl Barth's remark about the bible and the newspaper. The world which is symbolized by the newspaper exercises a control on our religious sensibilities. Human imagination cannot escape the present age, and neither can Jesus. To hear the word of God, the Christian has no choice except to face the world.

Facing the world is simply a way of describing the deliberate choice to stand with and for those who are economically and socially oppressed, which is often referred to as "the preferential option for the poor." This option expresses the deep change that occurs within someone which corresponds to the first beatitude, "Blessed are the poor in spirit" (Mt 5:3). A person is not born poor in spirit; a person becomes poor in spirit when in loyalty, affection, aspiration and action he or she determines freely and even joyfully to step inside the world of the poor "in spirit." For some, this determination may call for a physical relocation. For everyone it spells a revolution in one's whole way of thinking and deciding.[17]

The option for the poor represents a radical transformation of a person's thinking and seeing, the way he or she "reads" the world and converses with it. Furthermore, the option for the poor is not only a personal decision or option made once and for all. It consists of a steady, penetrating insight into the basic truth about us that we all come from God. It seeps into the tiniest cracks in our minds and hearts, changing the soul so profoundly that we begin to live, here and now, the reality of God's kingdom. The option for the poor represents real intellectual, spiritual and political space. One cannot see the constellation of stars known as the Southern Cross from the skies of the northern hemisphere. Similarly, one cannot read the sacred texts of our faith and both "look *and* perceive" in the matter of the secret of the kingdom of God (Mk 4:11–12) outside the world, or the social space, of the poor and oppressed.

The fourth gospel opens by referring to God's Word which "became flesh and lived among us" (Jn 1:14). Comparing the mystery of Christ (that is, what God has done for us in and through Jesus) to a word was an early Christian effort at interpreting the significance of the gospel. The ancient writer who hit upon this comparison was steeped in the Wisdom literature of the Hebrew scriptures. That author had, in effect, constructed a Christ symbol by giving us the idea of "the Word made flesh." The New Testament has many ways of expressing its faith in the risen Jesus, but the symbol of the Word made flesh stands out as particularly rich.

Now, may we do in our time what Paul and the evangelists did in theirs? Do we have the freedom to "reconstruct the Christ symbol" in order to address the circumstances, needs and spiritual hunger of the people of our day? I believe that we do. Whatever symbols we construct have to be consonant with the traditions we find in the New Testament. But the traditions are like trajectories. The church did not consider itself so bound to New Testament imagery and language that it could not introduce non-scriptural language into its creeds of the fourth and fifth centuries. And just as there are a variety of portraits of Jesus in the New Testament, so we can imagine that there would be a variety of ways to reconstruct the Christ symbol.[18]

The Word became flesh, the fourth gospel tells us: not just flesh in the abstract, of course, but an actual human being. Could it be that the preferential option for the poor is a present-day reformulation of that ancient Christian insight into the mystery of God in Christ? For the Word not only became flesh; it retained flesh. It not only entered the human story; it remains ever a part of our history. The flesh which the Word became was not just any flesh; it was flesh among the people of Israel, and it took the form of a slave (Phil 2:7), embracing human poverty (2 Cor 8:9). The Word, therefore, was slavery made flesh; it was poverty made flesh. And, we might add, it was oppression made flesh. Through that Word, God entered into a profound solidarity with the human race: not with humanity in the abstract, without any differentiations, but with humanity in a very concrete form.

God's identification with the people of Israel, we have already seen, was not a matter of divine racism. Israel represented the people of God in history, all of those who cry out to him for deliverance and hope in him for justice and peace. The flesh of suffering humanity is what God embraced, and every genuine expression of God's Word is going to bring us face to face with that reality.

5

The Place in Which We Pray

Saint Augustine was once asked by an extremely wealthy and pious widow about how she should pray. Noting that prayer is an activity most befitting Christian widows, he replied:

> The *destitution and desolation that widows experience* make them especially apt for this kind of work. All those who understand that *every heart is destitute and desolate in this world*, as long as it is on pilgrimage, away from the Lord, commit their "widowhood," so to speak, to God their protector, in unceasing, whole-hearted prayer. You must pray, then, as a widow of Christ, who doesn't yet see him whose help you implore. And though you are very well off, *pray as one who is poor*; you do not yet possess the true riches of the world to come, where you will have to fear no loss. Although you have children and grandchildren, and a large household, *pray as one who is desolate*: we cannot count on temporal blessings remaining to comfort us even to the end of this life.[1]

Augustine's answer is somewhat predictable. He draws on the notion of being poor and desolate in spirit because from the most basic point of view, that is, from the perspective of our common humanity, all of us are existentially poor. This basic truth should be enough to remind the widow, and indirectly all of us, how we stand before God.

Every Christian life becomes, therefore, a symbolic expression of the human condition itself. Even though she is rich, the woman is urged to stand before God in prayer as one who is truly poor since she has not yet attained the treasure of heaven. And although she is surrounded by prosperity and loved ones, she ought to come before God as one who is desperately alone. For she could conceivably lose what she has; besides, the good things of this life frequently fail to bring us the deeper happiness we inwardly desire.

Augustine's conviction that only in heaven will the heart's desire for blessedness be satisfied and his reminder about the transitory nature of the things of this world are hardly novel ideas. But are they helpful ones? Union with the poor and desolate is spiritualized; poverty and desolation become metaphors for the human condition itself. The consequence of this spiritualization is an asceticism which turns its back upon this world and through its counter-cultural ethos mounts a powerful critique of society.[2] Yet neither of these attitudes adequately correspond to what we know about Jesus' practice. Jesus did not lead a world-denying crusade, nor did he envision himself as a counter-cultural social reformer.

Suppose, however, Augustine had shaped his thoughts with less attention to the next life and more attention to this one. Suppose he had taken greater account of the actual poverty and the actual desolation which, say, the widows of his day were enduring. Or suppose, further, that he had turned their experience into a window on the wider world of human misery and suffering. He might then have encouraged the rich widow in this case to sell everything she owned and give it to the poor, as Jesus had once advised the rich man. But she was already an undeniably generous person, and Augustine may have realized that such radical counsel was probably not meant to be universalized. Or he might have helped her to understand that poverty and desolation were places where one needed to look in order to find God: not poverty and desolation as metaphors for the universal human condition, but as the concrete circumstances of the everyday world in which countless men and women are forced to live.

By choosing the latter course, Augustine would have avoided the difficulty of having to develop *two* spiritualities and two approaches to prayer, one for the rich and the other for the poor. For generosity and almsgiving are obviously not religious practices to be observed by the destitute. They are only applicable to those with disposable income and temporal goods. Nevertheless, however commendable and important it is, generosity cannot be the only requirement God places on the rich. The gospel does not give us permission to live out our faith and at the same time remain insulated from people who suffer physical desolation and poverty under the pretext that we are practicing "spiritual poverty." It cannot be the case that the powerful and well-to-do have to learn how to find God in their security and their affluence (which they never have to renounce), while the poor alone have to learn how to find God in actual poverty. The gospel does not provide a dual-highway to blessedness, one crafted for the rich and the other for the poor.

No; their paths must join, for there is one spirituality for both. If the poor must find God in their poverty, then the rich are not going to find God apart from them. Those who are socially and economically advantaged are not going to comprehend the God of Jesus unless they make an option for the poor. It may be worth recalling that this is by no means to be confused with an option for poverty, for poverty is destructive of human life and dignity.

In an essay entitled "The True Social Place of the Church," Ignacio Ellacuría, one of the Jesuits slain in El

Salvador in November 1989, wrote: "Social place does not mean where one normally is, the site where one lives, where one has one's address, or where one is registered." The idea is a major one, not just for the sake of our spirituality, but for the sake of the way we approach politics, social and economic realities, cultural life, and so on. The place where we physically reside is not necessarily the place ("the space") inhabited by our affections, interests and loyalties. Unless we understand this truth about ourselves, the real motives behind our actions and decisions will remain concealed.

The person who lives in very modest circumstances but who constantly dreams of being rich and famous is courting frustration and depression. A tension, if not an open contradiction, exists between physical place and social space. Such people share, vicariously, the values of an elite which they most likely will never join. The individual who enjoys the very highest standard of living, and who, out of genuine humanitarian interest, contributes to various charities, has not thereby discharged his or her Christian responsibility to those on the bottom. For the possibility of amassing fortunes raises crucial questions about economic systems which allow some people to amass fortunes and power while countless others remain mired in poverty and despair. The doors which open so easily and widely to some of us slam shut for the vast majority of the world. Therefore, the fact that one contributes to worthy causes does not mean that one has entered the social space of the poor. Ellacuría continues:

> Jesus, for example, went out to many places. He could dine with the rich, he could spend the night at Lazarus' house, he could go up the mountain and preach on the lake, preach in Galilee, or struggle in Judea and Jerusalem—but in his mind, his heart, and his practice he placed himself with the most needy. Of

course I know that it can most correctly be stated that Jesus was with God, his Father, but one thing does not exclude the other. First, being-in and being-with are not the same: Jesus was located in that social place constituted by the poor, *and it was from that place, which purified and enlightened his heart, that he was with God and went about his Father's business.* Second, *this very being with God was not unrelated to his being with the poor,* among whom he wished to establish his dwelling.[3]

What Ellacuría said here stands in marked contrast to what we saw in Augustine. Needless to say, I am not faulting Augustine on his advice; I am only pointing out an intrinsic limitation of a view of prayer and spirituality which does not take our present history seriously enough. For Ellacuría and others, being in the social place of the poor (which is not necessarily the physical place where one lives) is an indispensable condition for leading a life today which is truly grounded in the gospel. In addition, that social place was where Jesus' own understanding of God was "purified and enlightened" and it remains the only place where his followers today will fully encounter the God of Jesus.

How does one enter that place? Whether we speak (with the Latin American church) of making a "preferential option" for the poor, or (with John Paul II) of a lived "solidarity" with the poor, or (with John S. Dunne) of "passing over" into the world of the poor, one thing is certain. We have to *do* something.[4] One does not learn patience, for example, or compassion from merely watching television, or reading a spiritual book. At some point we have to meet the people who constitute the social place known as the world of the poor. For many of us this sort of undertaking is fraught with fear. The unknown can be a terrifying prospect. Inserting oneself into a situation where one knows oneself to be treading on unfamiliar territory, or where one is not in control, is bad enough. But to allow, not to mention *encourage*, those who are close to us and whom we love dearly to set foot on strange ground may be even worse.

Christian faith has a model for this type of insertion into a different world in one of its early understandings of Jesus:

> For you know the generous act of our Lord Jesus Christ, that though he was rich, yet for your sakes he became poor, so that by his poverty you might become rich. (2 Cor 8:9)

Paul's reason for appealing to the generosity of Jesus was to encourage the Corinthian community to give unstintingly in the face of the pressing needs of Christians living in Jerusalem. He also recalled for the Corinthians the communities of Macedonia which, while enduring extreme poverty themselves, had donated beyond what they could afford. Indeed, Paul writes, the Christians of Macedonia even begged him "for the privilege of sharing in this ministry to the saints" (2 Cor 8:4). Here we have an instance, therefore, of people who, though poor, became even poorer for the sake of others still less fortunate.

But the example Paul was drawing on was that of Christ. What Christ's riches consisted of, or his generosity, Paul does not tell us; he certainly does not mean that Jesus had been born into wealth. It is possible that he was presupposing the imagery we find in another letter:

> who, though he was in the form of God
> > did not regard equality with God
> > as something to be exploited.
> but emptied himself,
> > taking the form of a slave,
> > being born in human likeness.
> > > (Phil 2:6–7)

If this was the idea Paul had in mind, then Christ's riches presumably had something to do with his standing outside of the human circle, beyond its fallenness, together with Adam before the great sin. The imagery here reveals more about very early reflection on the mystery of Christ than it does about Jesus himself. The Corinthian text implies that all of us, with whom Jesus entered into solidarity, are actually poor. The fact is, however, that we do not live in real poverty, unless Paul intended to equate being sinful with being poor.

Nevertheless, the importance of Paul's thought as he encouraged the Corinthians to give generously lies in its application to everyday life. If Christ inserted himself into our condition so completely that he became actually poor, then what prevents us from inserting ourselves into the situation of our brothers and sisters who are poorer than we are? Indeed, the Macedonians must have done something just like that, as we see from their response to the news of their fellow Christians in need.

Next, we have to ask whether we are *afraid* to have contact with the world of those "below" us, that unfamiliar place where we encounter the other who is less educated, less cultured, less well-spoken, less religious perhaps, less informed, less well dressed, less acquainted with hard work, less likely ever to get ahead, and more likely to require public assistance, or to be using food stamps, or to contract AIDS, or to be arrested. Such a place is going to expose not only our fears, but our assumptions and prejudices as well. For many of us, that social place is not where we would choose to be even for a brief time, and certainly not where we would choose to spend our lives.

To suggest that we do not have to *dwell* in that place in order to *be* in that space may be somewhat disingenuous. It could sound like the permission we have been waiting for all along, namely, to do some good without making any major changes in the way we live, do business, carry on our routines, and so forth. The problem is not that we cannot serve God *and* make money, because all of us do exactly that. Rather, the difficulty is that sometimes what we have to do in order to make money, or the kind of person we have to become in order to keep making it, drives a wedge between us and our neighbor. The good we accomplish with one hand gets undone by the other hand, especially if that other hand is the one driving the wedge.[5]

The Awkwardness of Crossing Over

I would like to draw on two recollections as a way of illustrating why entering a different social space can be intimidating. Some years ago a wealthy but eccentric widow invited me to lunch. She lived alone in an enormous old house, with twelve dogs of various breeds and sizes. The dining room table was set with costly china and gold-plated knives and forks, crystal goblets and sterling silver serving trays. On the table sat a tenderloin roast at least eighteen inches long, a dressed turkey, a baked ham, lobster salad, assorted vegetables and dinner rolls, and two shrimp cocktails, one at either end of the long table. A large basket of fruit sat on the sideboard, along with three pies and a great plate of cookies. I gasped. All that food, I asked, for two people? She explained that part of her monthly allowance came in the form of groceries, because her husband had been in the food business. Fearing that she might have offended me by preparing so much food, she asked me if I thought it was too much. When I replied, yes, that it did strike me as a little excessive for lunch, she went outside into the neighborhood and invited as many children she could round up to join us. In short order we were about fourteen. More china was set out, more linen napkins, more gold plate.

The youngsters were overawed by the setting, and they were obviously not used to the niceties of fine dining. Although they warmed to the food quickly enough and went home loaded with the leftovers, they never appeared completely comfortable during the meal. One was afraid to use the fork, lest she scratch one of the exquisitely colored plates. They were all afraid of soiling the linen napkins.

The second recollection goes back to an evening shortly after I was ordained, when I was called upon to celebrate mass in a tiny village in northern India. The missioner with whom I was staying had fallen sick, and the mass had been planned for several months. The people, who were just a tiny pocket of Catholics in an overwhelmingly Hindu country, were counting on this public expression of their religious identity. To cancel mass at the last minute would have meant their losing face. Someone had to go.

The village consisted of a cluster of huts. There was neither electricity nor running water, neither paved road nor sidewalk. A narrow footpath wound through a maze of fields and hamlets, largely Hindu and, like the small community of Christians, extremely poor. After mass, I was invited into the hut of the chief catechist. A kerosene lantern lit the tiny room. On the table the family had placed a hard-boiled egg, a bowl of rice, a glass of very sweet milk tea, and half an orange. They had even managed to buy a small cake about the size of a macaroon, coated with honey, the kind I had seen each day in the bazaar crawling with bees and flies. I said, in English, to the sister who had accompanied me that I really was not hungry. She answered, calmly but firmly, that I had to eat, that this was more food than the family would share in a day, and that if I refused I would be insulting my host, who sat across from me with his wife and children, smiling and urging me with signs to begin. The family would have their tea together afterward.

Both of these memories bring out for me some of the feelings we can have when moving into a different space. It is awkward for the poor to step into the homes of the rich, and it is equally disconcerting for the rich to enter the homes of the poor. The poor, coming from a different social class, feel out of place and may not know what etiquette is expected of them. When the rich walk into the homes of the poor, they might feel equally out of place, and guilty as well. I did. Would the food spread out on the table exhaust the family's supply for a week? Was the glass washed? What about the flies on the dessert? And whose hands had sectioned the fruit? Could there be lice on the stained cushion on which I sat?

Looking back on that scene now, I am embarrassed over the way I reacted: my nervousness, my preoccupation with contracting a tropical disease, but most of all my sense that somehow I was above those people. I was in their place, but I had not entered the world of their social space. In my head I knew that we were all children of God. In my stomach, however, I could feel both the resistance and reassurance that come with privilege. We certainly were not meeting as equals because I was not able to permit that, and neither were the people. They knew that the foreigner could never really be one of them; so did I. And that mutual awareness made me feel strangely safe.

When the Christian story speaks about Christ becoming poor for our sake, it is saying that Jesus was not an outsider walking temporarily within the world of the poor. He really belonged there. Indeed, although Jesus occasionally dined in the homes of the rich, one can wonder just how comfortable he felt there, for the gospel suggests that there was a certain awkwardness about some of those meals. In one case, a "woman in the city who was a sinner" barged into the house of a Pharisee where Jesus was eating. The Pharisee was immediately sensitive to this breach of social distance; she had no place in his home (Lk 7:36ff).

On another occasion, also in the house of a Pharisee, Jesus offended his host because he had neglected to wash before starting to eat (Lk 11:37ff). And on yet another occasion Jesus was on the way to share a meal with a Pharisee, on a sabbath, when he was confronted by a man with dropsy. Jesus had not even made it to the dinner table before the unpleasantness began (Lk 14:1). And then, of course, one of the great complaints against Jesus was that he "welcomes sinners and eats with them" (Lk 15:2).

In each instance, the shock can be traced to the fact that Jesus broke social barriers. The scandal was essentially a matter of mixing two different classes of people. The rich and righteous did not cross over into the world of the uninstructed poor, and the defenseless poor did not cross the threshold into the world of the cultured, pious and secure rich.

Yet it is not helpful to portray the rich as villains. I certainly did not feel as if I had failed morally when I reacted as I did in that Indian village. One has to learn. One has to be helped to see how limited his view of the world is and how easily we become paralyzed by vague fears and suspicions. Money belts, anti-theft devices, security systems, identification codes, closed-circuit cameras, alarms, electric fences…there are sound reasons why we have devised such things, but what does this constant attention to being secure reveal about what we have become as a society? We have become obsessed with taking precautions. And whom are we protecting ourselves against? The stranger, the foreigner, the immigrant, is no longer simply someone we do not know, but a potential threat to our way of life. The people outside the gate who have no title to our privileges make us nervous. For me, the "other" was simply that poor family who sat across from me, happy and grateful that a mass had been celebrated in their village, on the window sill of their home, while I was worried about the flies that might have lighted on a leper's sore, or an infant's runny nose. My head told me that we were connected, related. My insides longed for the protection of window screens and boiled water. No; my insides really wanted to be as far away from that spot as possible!

There is a certain awkwardness, indeed, even a strangeness involved in crossing over from one social or economic class to another. Cultural crossovers may be somewhat easier. Even if we cannot become fully integrated into another cultural world, at least we can stand before that world with a certain degree of admiration and respect. Encountering a different culture is not so mentally and spiritually taxing as walking into an economic world which is either very much above or very much below the one we have been accustomed to.

I readily acknowledge that the complex social and economic problems confronting us today cannot be resolved so easily as sitting at table with poor people. But something might at least begin there, at least in the way that we pray. The only way to confirm or disconfirm the value of Jesus' teaching

> But when you give a banquet, invite the poor, the crippled, the lame, and the blind. And you will be blessed (Lk 14:13–14)

is to experiment with the truth of his words. Religious belief which leaves us with all answers and no questions, which helps us to cope with history but protects us from being engaged by its "underside," which never gets the rich man to cross over to Lazarus' side of the city, is bound to fail us sooner or later. The Pharisee of the gospel who was incapable of seeing the world from below had sentenced himself to roaming endlessly in the emptiness of a barren temple, a temple as large as the universe, but cold and lifeless. What God would hear him there when he prayed? For God was among the people, the very ones whom the gates were supposed to keep safely outside.

Praying with Determination: A Second Widow Story

With his characteristic attentiveness to the importance of prayer in Christian life, Luke begins chapter 18 of his gospel with the parable of a persistent widow: "Then Jesus told them a parable about their need to pray always and not to lose heart" (Lk 18:1). The widow, who lived "in a certain city," had most likely been done a severe injustice, perhaps over a settlement regarding her deceased husband's estate. Consequently, she approaches a judge who turns out to be both dishonest and godless, and lacking in the most elementary human compassion.[6]

For the evangelist, that widow served to exemplify an important disposition of a Christian before God. Luke hardly meant to imply that God in any way resembles the unjust judge, of course.[7] A widow standing alone before a crooked judge could never parallel the situation of a believer before God. In the end, the unscrupulous judge decided he had more to lose than to win if he sided with his wealthy patrons instead of the poor widow, and he ruled in her favor. The gospel does not reveal what specifically the widow did. Had she rallied the help of all the other widows of that city and organized a protest against the corrupt judge? Had she caused him public embarrassment by hounding the magistrate as he made his way through the market place, or whenever he left his house? Whatever she did, it was enough to make him relent.

As an instruction about prayer, the point of the parable might well be that God joins sides with the exploited and impoverished widows of this world in their efforts to secure justice. After all, why would any of us persist in prayer, unless we were convinced that God was on our side? Luke appears to be suggesting that God habitually stands with the poor, urging and empowering them to fight back against institutions and structures, individuals and groups, which would ignore them, cheat them, or even try to convince them to remain passive in the face of abuse. In short, poor widows ought not to acquiesce but to resist and to fight, because God has taken their side against the unjust judges of this world and against whatever public policies, financial arrangements, or bureaucracies an "unjust judge" might represent. In the pulpits of the poor, this parable is certainly reassuring good news.

Yet by proposing this widow as an example of the prayer of persistence, Luke has in effect instructed all of us about the place from which we pray. Clearly, Jesus could have employed any number of illustrations of being persistent. A child that keeps asking its parents for something to eat (Lk 11:11), a merchant who keeps looking for the pearl of great price (Mt 13:45), a housekeeper who keeps sweeping and searching to locate a lost coin (Lk 15:8), even a shepherd who refuses to rest until he finds his lost sheep (Lk 15:3): all of these could have served as examples of prayerful persistence. Thus to select the example of an exploited widow taking on a corrupt judge colors this particular instruction about prayer considerably.

The woman was not just persistent and determined. She was also vigorous, bold, even aggressive in the face of having been defrauded of what was rightfully hers. Christians at prayer, we should conclude, always stand alongside people like her in their unrelenting pursuit of justice and dignity. The God who steadies poor widows as they struggle against their adversaries is a God in solidarity with the world. The widow's persistence points the rest of us toward growing in prayerful solidarity. Jesus' story about her is yet another invitation to think about the place from which we pray.

6

All Petitions Lead to the Center

We always pray out of our incompleteness; it is impossible not to. Sometimes we are aware of just how incomplete we are, many times we are not. In either case, that very incompleteness is what prompts our petitions to God. If we already possessed everything we needed or wanted, we would ask for nothing. If we experienced no interior deficiency, no sense of apartness between ourselves and other human beings, or between ourselves and the material universe, no estrangement even from our own selves, then we might never pray at all. The humble prayer of petition and the intense spiritual longing of the mystic for union with God tap into the same reality within the human soul. For in our souls we know that we are not yet all that we have been created to be. Human beings by themselves and without God are radically unstable, and consequently so too are the world and the societies in which they live.

In short, not only are we incomplete as individuals; we are also incomplete corporately, as a race and as a world. For that reason, just as the Spirit prays from within us when we do not know what to ask for, so too all of creation groans for redemption and liberation. In our turn, through our prayer as well as through our practice, we give utterance to creation's desire for justice, peace, deliverance and wholeness.

Most treatments of prayer devote some attention to the prayer of petition, since this is probably the most common form of praying. Many devout people sincerely believe that God has answered their prayers. Such has been their experience as well as the testimony of countless Christians before us, and that experience and testimony deserve to be respected. The New Testament voices are unequivocal on the point that God hears and answers our requests.[1]

At the same time, petitionary prayer raises the most conceptual difficulties for us. One difficulty is that in the experience of other equally devout people prayers appear not to have been really answered; their requests were seldom granted. Why then do we continue to ask God for things? On this score, the gospel itself may have misled us when it says, "Ask, and it will be given." Another difficulty is that petitionary prayer raises all sorts of theological questions about the will of God. Is God's plan for us already determined? Can we honestly hope to influence or even to change the divine will in our regard? Are some petitions more fitting or more welcome in God's sight than others? If God loves us like a parent, why is it even necessary to ask for the things which God already knows we need?

Any answer to these questions would have to be speculative at best, but in the matter of praying speculation about God is not very satisfying. In the long run, all we can say is that every Christian prayer proceeds from a profound desire to see creation reach its fulfillment. "Your will be done" does not represent a docile submissiveness to forces outside of our control, but a very deep longing for the full redemption or liberation of all things. "Your will be done" also pledges our full cooperation in the process of that liberation. What we see by way of preview in the resurrection of Jesus is what we eagerly want for all creation, namely, wholeness or completion. We want everything to be finally joined to God, and this wanting lies behind every request we make in our prayers, no matter how insignificant the concern or how silent the petition.

"Ask, and It Will Be Given": Was Jesus Serious?

Petitionary prayer is often the mark of simple, everyday piety. We ask God for strength to get through a day, or to deal with some particular crisis, or even to locate an object we misplaced. We pray for good weather, for success in our endeavors, and for the health and prosperity of our family and friends. Underlying such prayer is an everyday faith that is neither so naive as to think that God will facilitate every least detail of our lives and spare us every possible inconvenience, nor so amorphous as to believe that a God who creates universes is totally uninterested in the tiny particulars of our daily existence.

In many instances we probably underestimate the inner resources with which God has endowed us. We look to God for help when God has already empowered us to obtain what we need or to resolve our difficulties. Sometimes petitionary prayer resembles the insecurity of a child grabbing hold of its mother's hand even when it can walk by itself.

In other instances, however, petitionary prayer has less to do with specific requests we make of God and more to do with ventilating in God's presence our anxieties, fears, loneliness, insecurity and love for others. We certainly do want things, but the prayer itself may actually be a symbolic expression of a deep religious hope that all will be well. Perhaps the spirit of petitionary praying is best summed up in Paul's confident words: "We know that all things work together for good for those who love God" (Rom 8:28). It is not so much the asking but the faith and hope which lie underneath that we need to attend to if we are to understand the prayer of petition.

It was Luke who recorded for us Jesus' teaching about persevering in our prayer. The well-known gospel text sounds almost romantic in its simplicity and innocence. But is Jesus' instruction readily confirmed by our experience?

> "So I say to you, Ask, and it will be given you; search, and you will find; knock, and the door will be opened for you. For everyone who asks receives, and everyone who searches finds, and for everyone who knocks, the door will be opened. Is there anyone among you who, if your child asks for a fish, will give him a snake instead of a fish? Or if the child asks for an egg, will give a scorpion? If you then, who are evil, know how to give good gifts to your children, how much more will the heavenly Father give the Holy Spirit to those who ask him!" (Lk 11:9–13)

Lurking here is the discrepancy most of us have noticed between these wonderful words from the gospel and the reality of not receiving what we have asked for. Looking at the faces of people one Sunday morning as they stood and listened so attentively to this passage, I wondered what might be passing through their minds. I spot a family with a son in prison, and another with a sister-in-law dying of AIDS. Another family, poor and hardworking, has entered the country illegally and lives under the constant fear of being found out and deported. A young father in the back pew recently lost his job. A grandmother has been beseeching heaven that her daughter's marriage will not break apart, while another couple still grieves over the death of an infant son. Each of us in the church picks up on the note of innocent confidence in that gospel reading and wonders what is wrong with us. Desperate requests for divine help have not been answered and no one seems to be able to explain why.

Some people might tell us that we have not prayed with sufficient faith, that is, with the faith that could command a mountain to fling itself into the sea (Mk 11:23). But this sort of explanation really amounts to an accusation; it leaves us feeling inadequate, even guilty over the poverty of our faith. The fault thereby becomes ours when requests are not granted.

Others will tell us that perhaps we have not prayed with the proper disposition, that is, with the compliant attitude of Jesus when he prayed, "not my will but yours be done" (Lk 22:42). If we have not been given what we asked for, then obviously it was not God's will that our request be granted.

There is some truth here, of course. Many things we desire might not ultimately be in our best interests, or in the best interests of those on whose behalf we are praying, although from our present standpoint we may not see why. But for several reasons this explanation is likewise weak. First, adult faith is not blind faith; it cannot be compared to giving God a blank check. God may be both all wise and all knowing, but that does not excuse us from the struggle involved in making holy, intelligent and informed choices. And second, it is simply untrue to say that whatever we have not received would not have been in our best interests. Such an assertion could never be proven. If we do not receive what we have asked for, and if what we have asked for is, so far as we can discern, both good and proper, there is no ground for asserting that God, foreseeing the future, has spared us the harm that would result if our request were granted. For example, if someone close to us dies instead of recovers, would anyone argue that God, foreseeing that the individual once recovered would later commit a terrible crime, has actually spared us heavier suffering? We can imagine lots of variations on this sort of explanation, all of them equally senseless. If God is capable of bringing about a recovery, God could certainly inspire a person later to avoid falling into sin.

Still others might suggest that our prayers often remain unanswered because we might not have prayed long enough. They could remind us, say, of the example of Saint Monica who prayed tearfully over many years for the moral conversion of her son Augustine. Or our friends might urge us to strengthen our prayer with penitential practice and additional good works. Finally, a few will chide us for having petitioned God at all. They will recall for us Jesus' words about not worrying, for example, about what we are to eat, or to wear, or to drink (Lk 12:22–31). If we *really* trusted God, then we would ask for nothing! We would realize that God already knows our needs, and that God, being good, will take care of them: "Instead, strive for his kingdom, and these things will be given you as well."

Let us consider these possibilities. While we would not gainsay the example of a persistent and saintly mother like Monica, some requests need to be answered speedily; twenty or thirty years would be too long a stretch. Besides, what sort of God would withhold the grace of conversion? Why should it even be necessary for us to ask, for example, that God lead someone back to the church? Or was it Monica herself as a person of faith who was Augustine's great grace? Might the same be true of us? Through our faithfulness and patience, do we become the grace which the person needs for whom we pray, the answer both to our prayer and to theirs?

And with respect to the gospel passage about not worrying, to whom was Jesus addressing himself? He certainly was not speaking to the poor. They could not have been the ones he had in mind when he continued, "Sell your possessions and give alms" (Lk 12:33). In other words, it would have been absolutely naive for Jesus to tell the poor not to worry about where their next meal would come from. Freedom from worry and anxiety is a spiritual indulgence for those whose fortunes are well invested or whose income is secure.

Finally, other friends might assure us that our prayer could very well have been answered, although in a way we had not anticipated. A person might ask God for riches, for instance, as a means to happiness, and eventually discover real contentment in service, commitment, and getting by on modest means, without being consciously aware of the interior change. In other words, sometimes we receive what we need, even when that does not correspond to what we may have asked for.

Proposing that our prayers may have been answered in indirect ways does help to resolve two concerns. First, it rescues our conviction that no prayer goes unheard: "Whatever you ask for in prayer with faith, you will receive" (Mt 21:22). Second, it enables us to see that not everything we ask for matters as greatly to God as it does to us. Nevertheless, one thinks of how the friends of Job annoyed God when they responded to Job's misfortune as if they were self-appointed press agents out to safeguard the divine honor. Are those who would offer us the round-about solution, namely, that all prayers are heard but many are answered indirectly, putting themselves in the role of Job's friends? Why did they feel compelled to rush to God's defense? In the same way we could ask whether some explanations of the merit of petitionary prayer are basically feeble human efforts to ward off a terrifying inse-curity. After all, if God cannot be counted on to grant our requests, then what is the value of continuing to believe?

As we can see, it is hard to locate a reliable explanation for why good prayers are frequently not answered. Any Christian who has tried to support acquaintances, friends, family members and loved ones during moments of crisis or tragedy, or in periods of grave economic and social turmoil, will appreciate the problem here. Why therefore should we ask God for anything? After watching so much suffering from around the world night after night on our television screens, who of us would not want to put God on trial, or at least to be given some answer to why we should bring our concerns before God at all? Praying itself is eminently sensible. There are, after all, other forms of prayer, such as thanksgiving and praise. But what about making requests of God?

The passage from Luke about trusting God was very likely written with reasonably well-to-do people in view. The spiritual advice Luke offered was not intended for the poor and the oppressed. Those people would probably have been asking God for deliverance from their enemies and from the hand of all who hated them (Lk 1:71), for redress from wrongs (Lk 1:52–53), for justice (Lk 18:7), even for scraps of food (Lk 16:21). With that in mind, Jesus' words about not being anxious over food and clothing have a context. But we should also go one step further.

As we already pointed out, in voicing our needs and desires we are expressing our conviction that God is concerned about *us*, even when some of the things we talk about in our prayer are trivial and inconsequential. Here the saying about the very hairs of our head being numbered should come to mind (Lk 12:7), for within it lies the intuition that even the most intimate details of our lives are known to God.

Nevertheless, even in the case of those things which

are of greater moment we do not expect, as adults, that God is going to alter the course of history, or the workings of the world, in response to us. Such an expectation would be unrealistic, immature and somewhat presumptuous. Tales of miracles, like requests for supernatural signs, pose a real threat to immature faith, as the apostle Thomas learned. For Thomas asked for a sign to steady his wavering faith, and he was told that believing cannot be tied to the granting of signs (Jn 20:24–29). The petitions we make to God *sometimes* represent our attempts to grapple with the tensions and suffering of life itself. To whom else can we go in moments of crisis and tragedy, except to God? Asking God for what we want or need thus becomes an expression of the basic trust in God's providence which sustains us from one day to the next. The important thing about such prayer may not be the request itself but our giving voice to the underlying belief that God would never abandon us.[2]

Belief in the abiding faithfulness of God is particularly strong and remarkable in the case of the poor. They may survive with "daily bread" or they may starve. They may finally receive justice against their adversaries or they may be arrested and killed. But the answer to their prayer for deliverance rarely comes speedily. Their lives are not going to improve without vast social, political and economic changes; and they might have to endure terrible suffering before they reach their promised land. God does not work painless, extraordinary wonders to hasten the day of freedom. If anything, God's ways seem to be characteristically slow. Indeed, God has taken the side of the poor in the slow, revolutionary processes of history which bring food to the chronically hungry, liberty to slaves, dignity to the oppressed, bold speech to the lips of the voiceless. God is present among them like a permanent endowment in their thirst for justice, in their struggle to bring about political change, in their hunger and in their poverty.

The one group which could legitimately be excused for abandoning faith in God would be the people who have been forced to live and die as victims of economic and social tyrannies, in other words, men and women forced into the underside of history. Paradoxically, however, sometimes that is where faith is the strongest. One reason why the bible is such a remarkable book is that it contains the testimony of people who endured slavery and persecution, poverty and exile, yet would not abandon hope in the divine promise.

Was Jesus serious about our persisting in the petitions we make to God? Or to phrase the question more accurately, was *the evangelist* for real when he placed those words on Jesus' lips? I believe Luke was.

The gospel writer shared the conviction that whatever good happens in our lives or in our world comes from God, and that the evil things which happen (although why they happen remains something we may never figure out theologically) cannot thwart God's overall designs. When Paul wrote that verse we cited above about all things working together for good for those who love God, he was not stating a new or recently discovered truth. He was drawing on a conviction that had been conceived in the long historical experience of suffering humanity and which was accepted as part of the inherited wisdom of the people of God.

Luke was serious about trusting God, but the teaching on prayer which he left us may need to be balanced by other dimensions of Christian experience. If Luke 11:9–13 were the New Testament's only instruction about prayer, the passage would be woefully misleading. Thus we do not have here a general theorem on prayer, for the evangelist knew very well that God's relationship to the world was more complex than how a child might have imagined things. The memory of Jesus crucified forces us to grow up spiritually and to find an adult way to relate to God. There was nothing romantic about the fate which befell Jesus; whoever follows Jesus, radically, will learn that serving the kingdom of God usually exacts a price. Luke knew that.

It would be impossible to prove or to disprove whether God had brought something about in answer to human prayer. The enormous suffering which human beings have inflicted upon one another down through the ages, from the murder of Abel to the ethnic cleansing in Bosnia or Rwanda, should throw sufficient cold water on any warm, pious sentiments inspired by

> Are not five sparrows sold for two pennies? Yet not
> one of them is forgotten in God's sight (Lk 12:6)

or verses like this one. We shall never get anywhere trying to guess why God allowed some things to occur but not others, despite our fervent petitions. Perhaps in the end it is safer to say that we have our desires, wants and needs, and that in our spiritual tradition men and women have long felt comfortable expressing these desires before God in the form of prayerful requests. The fact that what we wanted came to pass does not mean that God favored us with a miracle or a special favor, while the fact that we failed to receive what we asked for does not imply that God did not hear us. The most consistent experience we share is our abiding sense that God is with us, despite the fact that requests have not been granted. Besides, the granting of requests is not the motive which leads us to continue relating ourselves consciously to God. We trust that in the long run things will be well, and we know that our conviction could not even get that far unless God had first taken hold of our hearts. The often quoted words of Julian of Norwich capture the intuition here:

> Thus the good Lord answered all the questions and doubts that I could produce. Most reassuringly he added, "I may make everything all right; I am able to; I intend to, and I shall. You will see for yourself that every sort of thing will be all right."[3]

Praying out of Our Incompleteness

The preceding remarks have been paving the way for us to see that all prayers of petition take us to a center. The reason why we have concerns, needs, wants and desires in the first place is that we are incomplete, unfinished, still in the process of being created. And not only are we incomplete, but all of creation as well:

> For the creation waits with eager longing for the revealing of the children of God; for the creation was subjected to futility, not of its own will but by the will of the one who subjected it, in hope that the creation itself will be set free from its bondage to decay and will obtain the freedom of the glory of the children of God; and not only the creation, but we ourselves...groan inwardly while we wait for adoption, the redemption of our bodies. (Rom 8:19–23)

The unfinished character of our lives, of our communities and societies, of our world and of our very history, is what makes petitioning God possible in the first place. For if we were already fully made, and if the world around us were already fully redeemed, we would need nothing, want nothing, seek nothing beyond what we had already attained. Thus all our requests to God proceed from the very nature of our incompleteness. Everything about us is unfinished, subjected to futility, and desirous of full redemption. Beneath every prayer of petition lies the request that God bring the work of creation to completion. In each of those prayers we are really imploring God for the gift of ultimate, definitive justice:

> Your kingdom come
> Your will be done,
>   on earth as it is in heaven.

Essentially there is only one petition that we make in the multiple intentions we speak to God. Indeed, we are heavily invested in many things, perhaps even worried and distracted, as Martha was, bringing all those worries and distractions into our conversation with God. But only one thing is finally necessary, and our desire for that one thing lies underneath all the concerns and worries of our lives. It even lies underneath a mother's constant prayer for her children, or a husband's daily prayer for his wife, since the love that prompts those prayers is large enough to embrace a world and will not be satisfied until it does. All creation groans, Paul wrote, for liberation and redemption; that must include us. In the moment when we realize the nature and the scope of the human heart's profound, not-to-be-silenced desire for full liberation, we shall have moved to the center from which every prayer is spoken. It is that desire which unites us with the whole human race, because the same desire cries from all of us in one form or another: Resurrection!

But while all of us share that yearning for deliverance, that desire acquires its most intense utterance on the lips of those who long for bread, for justice, for an end to violence, for freedom. Thus it is not just a common desire for blessedness which unites us, but a particular form of human desire, namely, the thirst for that justice, righteousness and communion which Jesus named the kingdom of God. Whenever our prayer is in touch with that core desire, we are praying from the center. The more solidarity becomes the mark of our interior lives, the more forcefully does the world itself teach us what to be asking for whenever we pray. Solidarity with the world universalizes our concerns and confers a distinctive shape on Christian prayer.

7

Prayer and the Resurrection: Facing a World Remade

Few gospel stories can match Luke's great parable about the two disciples on the road to Emmaus for its power to console, reassure and illumine people whose faith might be wavering and whose prayer feels barren. When the heart feels empty and the soul feels the chill of disillusion, through that wonderful encounter with an unrecognized Christ Luke's voice and faith reach across centuries and cultures to quicken and renew our religious imaginations. That parable captured a timeless moment within the interior life of the ancient church. And ever after, in the breaking open of the word and the sharing of the bread, Christians would recover one of the primitive and foundational elements of the Easter experience. The Emmaus story still has the power to remake daily existence. It enables us to see the familiar and the ordinary with graced freshness, to discover splendor and mystery where before we had been tasting boredom, disappointment and failure.

But there is another story, equally powerful in the way it grabs hold of our hearts and imaginations; another story which likewise has the power to remake the way we view the world. It is the episode in John's gospel when Thomas encountered the risen Jesus. To appreciate the richness of that moment, it is essential to recall that Thomas was the disciple who had told the others that they should all accompany Jesus as he returned to a place of great danger: "Let us also go, that we may die with him" (Jn 11:16). Thomas was prepared to be with Jesus under whatever circumstances, even if doing so should cost him his life! This is hardly the hesitant, cautious faith of someone who came to be referred to as "doubting Thomas."

Having learned the news of the resurrection from the other disciples, Thomas was indeed waiting to have his faith in Jesus confirmed. He wanted to touch the marks of Jesus' crucifixion. Perhaps in his soul Thomas was just starting to comprehend the mysterious link between death and life, between cross and resurrection. Jesus risen, Thomas learned, would always bear the marks of his crucifixion. In Thomas' case, recognizing Jesus would mean learning to discern Jesus in men and women of every time and place, not just in Judea or in Galilee, who bore the marks of crucifixion. Thomas, after all, had been ready to die with Jesus. Now, perhaps, he was learning that one can also die with Jesus by living and dying alongside his sisters and brothers.

Thomas' final, prayerful exclamation "My Lord and my God!" (Jn 20:28) may have been as much a declaration of mystery as it was an expression of belief in Jesus risen. One wonders what Saul's reaction might have been when he heard the words, "Saul, Saul, why do you persecute *me*?" (Acts 9:4), or the reaction of the righteous in the final judgment scene when they asked, "Lord, when was it that we saw *you* hungry...?" and then heard the king's reply, "Truly I tell you, just as you did it to one of the least of these who are members of my family, you did it to *me*" (Mt 25:40). In each instance, the surprise came from realizing that Jesus had identified with the crucified ones of history. Or to state things more pointedly, the insight came from viewing poverty, hunger, oppression, betrayal, exploitation, desperation, persecution and so forth, as marks of crucifixion. Is there any wonder that Thomas would have made his exclamation? He had just discovered the great truth of the gospel: the story of Jesus was really a story about God. The world would never look the same way again; Thomas' imagination had just been transformed.

From the figure of Thomas we grasp yet another dimension of the Christian experience of Jesus risen. To stand with the crucified one where he is, wherever in the world we perceive the marks of his crucifixion, *and not be afraid*: that is Easter. And why would we not be afraid? For the simple reason that God is there. Experiencing God there, in and alongside the crucified ones, is consummately an Easter grace.

Resurrection Is More Than Just a Proof

The clearest evidence that Jesus has been raised from the dead has to be the Christian community itself when that community is fully living the gospel. Nothing is so persuasive as joyful, courageous witness. It has often been said that the gospel of Mark is actually a long passion story with an extended introduction. It might be more accurate to say that the gospel is one long Easter story, not only because Easter faith suffuses the whole gospel from beginning to end, but also because every experience of the cross simultaneously includes an awareness of God's presence. The same hand which raised Jesus from the dead is present in every single gospel scene, empowering, guiding, blessing, healing. If a major element of the Easter narratives at the end of the gospels is the experience of coming to recognize the features of Jesus risen, then the paschal dimension of the entire gospel must surely be our coming to recognize the features of God across the whole of Jesus' ministry. Recognition is everything, as Jesus once reminded his adversaries:

> But if it is by the finger of God that I cast out the demons, then the kingdom of God has come to you. (Lk 11:20)

Over time, the resurrection of Jesus came to mean different things to different people. For some, the resurrection was proof positive of Jesus' identity as Son of God. For others, it was divine confirmation of the existence of another life, God's way of proving

> that those who die for the sake of God live to God, as do Abraham and Isaac and Jacob and all the patriarchs. (4 Macc 16:25)

For still others, the raising of Jesus from the dead represented divine approval of Jesus' teaching about the kingdom of God and the victory of God's justice over the powers of sin and death, poverty and oppression. It might also have been viewed as God's way of rewarding Jesus for his obedience and perseverance.

In the eyes of many early Christians, the resurrection presaged that the end of the age was near and that all the righteous were about to be released from their graves (see Mt 27:52). On that score, needless to say, believers were mistaken. Yet central to every understanding of the resurrection was the conviction that, if Jesus had not been raised from the dead, then there would have been no story to tell, no proclamation of God's good news and no reason to keep the memory of Jesus alive. Paul's logic has endured through the ages: "and if Christ has not been raised, then our proclamation has been in vain and your faith has been in vain" (1 Cor 15:14).

The Easter story still rivets many people's attention on the glory which we all hope will follow this present earthly existence. This would be especially true of Christians whose lives have been scarred by suffering or persecution. Dwelling on this aspect of the message is understandable. For them, to think of Easter is to think of heaven.

Nevertheless, the hope to which the resurrection gives rise is not primarily the prospect of sharing eternal glory, even for martyrs. Hope has to be firmly centered on this world, for it is into this world that the risen Jesus sent his disciples. Belief in future glory, as Vatican II reminded us, can never become a warrant for ignoring or taking less seriously the heavy demands of the present. Quite the contrary, belief in the resurrection should bring great urgency to the way we lead our lives. Furthermore, it is belief in Jesus risen, not the possibility of his returning at the hour we least expect (Lk 12:40), which ought to keep the Christian community zealous, committed and focused.

Fear is not what motivates us to remain faithful: the fear of falling asleep, as the disciples did in the garden, or running out of oil, like the foolish virgins of the gospel parable, or being caught off-guard, like someone visited by a thief in the night. Life according to the gospel is marked by hope and joy, a freedom of spirit which no one can ever steal and a boldness that comes from standing with Jesus risen. The impact of the Easter story, therefore, should naturally be a deeper care and concern for this world. The more deeply one cares for this world and enters into solidarity with it, the more profound will be his or her grasp of why God raised Jesus from the dead.

Easter witnesses (which we are) will always read the problems of the present as possibilities for redemption.

Instead of beholding the world as a wilderness hostile to human life and gospel values, the Christian views the world as loved, as longing for deliverance and transformation. The world becomes a school in which the Spirit is continually teaching us about the mystery of God and the mission of love and hope that we have been called to share in. It becomes our Galilee, the everyday place in which Jesus meets us and continues his mission of proclaiming the kingdom and driving out demons (Mk 3:14–15).

The resurrection would be reduced to a story-book lesson about goodness paying off in the end, if we were to hear its central message as the promise of final reward. After all, the moral and spiritual life of a follower of Jesus is not driven by the desire or need for reward, or even by the need for divine affirmation, like the way we look to parents, teachers and other authority figures in our lives for approval. We are not religious adolescents craving the Father's approbation, and that was not the meaning of the resurrection for Jesus either. The Spirit had schooled him along much further than that. Countless men and women could testify that those who pursue the interior life because they are seeking great consolation or an experience of being loved by God should be prepared for a giant letdown. Not without reason does the contemplative tradition speak of a "dark night of the soul."

Although the resurrection is often presented as the *theoretical* justification for Christian faith, God's raising Jesus from the dead is not an abstract truth or the logical first principle of our religion. The resurrection does not refer to an idea but to an event. That event was neither the physical resuscitation of Jesus nor his being raised bodily and exalted to God's right hand. The raising of Jesus from the dead is the concrete, *experiential* foundation of the Christian way of life. As such, it refers to the liberating or saving action of God in our lives in and through our faith in Jesus.

There is no evidence anywhere in the New Testament that the risen Jesus was "seen" by anyone who did not already have a predisposition to faith. This was true of the women whose faith had brought them to the tomb to anoint Jesus' body. It was true of the disciples whose faith, though unsteady at times, kept them in Jesus' company and enabled them to join in his mission. Thomas may have found it hard to accept the report of the other disciples, but he could hardly be classified as an unbeliever. And Paul, the great persecutor, may have undergone a dramatic change, but it would be a mistake to think that there were no spiritual and psychological antecedents to his legendary conversion. Not only was Paul's faith in God fierce, but the strength and insight of that faith must have paved the way for his encounter with the risen Jesus.

So too in our case. Our association with others who are believers disposes us to recognize the risen Jesus when we encounter him. Even to recite the words "Jesus is risen" is to make a faith-statement. That claim is not an announcement of dry fact and it is not a neutral piece of historical information, but a declaration of hope and awareness of God's abiding presence in the world. "Jesus is risen" represents a conviction about the triumph of grace that originates within an experience of profound moral and spiritual empowerment, of great inner freedom, of being loved and forgiven, of being chosen and sent forth. The one who says "Jesus is risen" is speaking to us as a man or woman alive in the Spirit. Such a person looks at the world with very different eyes. For such a person Easter has remade the world.

The Resurrection as Experience of Salvation

The eminent Dutch theologian Edward Schillebeeckx opened the second volume of his monumental study on Jesus with these words:

> It began with an encounter. Some people—Aramaic-and perhaps also Greek-speaking Jews—came into contact with Jesus of Nazareth and stayed with him. This encounter, and what took place in the life of Jesus and in connection with his death, gave their personal lives new meaning and new significance. They felt that they had been born again, that they had been understood, and this new identity found expression in a similar solidarity towards others, their fellow-men. This change in the course of their lives was the result of their encounter with Jesus, for without him they would have remained what they had been (see 1 Cor 15:17). It had not come about through any initiative of their own; it had simply happened to them.[1]

Although Schillebeeckx does not state the point here in so many words, belief in the resurrection appears to have been a way of expressing the early church's *experience* of being saved. Whenever believers professed that Jesus had been raised from the dead, they were in effect claiming that God's saving grace had come to them in and through the crucified one. Within the perspective of Christian religious experience, resurrection and salvation are two sides of the same coin. A person's *faith* that Jesus has been raised from the dead is ultimately confirmed on the basis of an *experience* of salvation. This is hardly to challenge the unanimous testimony of the New Testament that God truly raised Jesus from the dead, but the resurrection involved considerably more than the bare fact that Jesus was now alive to God. Jesus, the gospel insists, is not to be found among the dead, *but among the living* (Lk 24:5).

What happened on that "first day of the week" needed to be interpreted, otherwise the news about Jesus being raised would have left people baffled at best and incredulous at worst. The term "Easter," we might say, could very well be the Christian shorthand for newness of life. *Salvation* was the interpretation of what took place on Easter, and there would be as many understandings of the resurrection as there were experiences of salvation. Our belief in the resurrection harbors a profound conviction about what God has done for the world in and through Jesus' life and death.

The raising of Jesus was not *primarily* a confirmation of the existence of an afterlife, for the afterlife was not in doubt for Jesus and his disciples. Such a sudden shift of divine attention to the afterlife would have undermined the direction and integrity of Jesus' ministry. The afterlife had not been central to his preaching; what was central was the kingdom of God as a possibility for this world.[2]

The raising of Jesus was not *primarily* God's way of rewarding Jesus for his obedience. There were many who had fully surrendered themselves to the will of God and persevered in their faith but whom God (so far as we know) had not raised from the dead. It would be impossible to argue that Jesus' faithfulness was more tested than anyone else's, and the fact is that by the time Jesus lived many had come to share the expectation that God would reward the righteous with everlasting life. *All* the righteous would be rewarded the same way.

Finally, the raising of Jesus from the dead was not meant *primarily* to be a revelation of Jesus' divine status. The first Easter witnesses were Jewish and firmly steeped in Israel's monotheism: "Hear, O Israel: The Lord is our

God, the Lord alone" (Deut 6:4). Any connection between Jesus and God which went beyond the familiar biblical category of adoption would not have immediately occurred to them. Speaking about the resurrection, Gerald O'Collins writes:

> In his transformed human existence Jesus became even more like unto God, as the Son in whom one can recognize even more fully the image of his Father (see Rom 1:3–4). His risen humanity reflects and resembles to the ultimate extent possible its divine cause. In the highest degree possible, through his risen life he participates in God (see Rom 6:10).[3]

What excited some early communities was the prospect that they would share Jesus' glory. They were confident that they, too, would participate in that same union with God. Jesus' being raised was a sign that if we also give ourselves to the reign of God here, God will raise us up. In other words, Jesus had not been raised for his own sake, but for ours. All of us would one day share the same divine inheritance.

If resurrection and salvation are so closely connected, then whatever meaningfulness we discover today in the raising of Jesus has to correspond to what we most hope for. If what we hope for most of all is life after death in the sense of personal immortality, then that will determine how we view the meaning of Easter. If what we are hoping for corresponds to the *new* heaven and new earth of the book of Revelation, then we will probably find in the raising of Jesus a pledge of divine faithfulness as we commit ourselves to fashioning an ever more humane world. If our hopes are largely social, political or economic, then the concrete form of those hopes will affect what we hear and celebrate in the raising of Jesus from the dead.

With the resurrection, we are dealing more with the transformation of Jesus' companions and followers than with Jesus himself, since we can only speculate about the nature of Jesus' present existence with God. And that transformation did not stop with the first disciples; it has continued to take place down through the centuries among those who fully and unreservedly immersed themselves in the story of Jesus.

Was the Resurrection Meant To Be Seen?

One of the most surprising details about the Easter stories is that none of Jesus' followers actually saw what happened early that "first day of the week" when Jesus was raised from the dead. Given the prominent place of signs throughout scripture, one would think that God would have made provision for at least someone to witness the event. The divine mystery has revealed itself through words *and* deeds, as Vatican II pointed out. God obviously wanted people to behold the parting of the Red Sea and the collapse of the walls of Jericho. The multiplication of the loaves and the raising of Lazarus would have been meaningless without witnesses. Why, then, for the foundational event of Christian faith did God not providentially arrange that spectators should be present? Of all God's mighty works, the raising of Jesus from the dead would have been the most spectacular. I think the answer is that the events of Easter morning were not meant to be seen, and had someone actually been posted nearby to watch the tomb, he would have witnessed nothing.[4]

The raising of Jesus was not what we would call a physical event, and certainly not an "historical" event in the ordinary sense of the word, as numerous commentators have pointed out. If the body of Jesus had simply been resuscitated, then his return to life would have been an event which people in principle could have witnessed. There would have been something actually to see. But that is not what happened. The risen Jesus stepped more deeply than ever into the lives of his followers, although the degree of his entry was contingent upon their readiness to believe.

A tree falling in the forest is a physical event. No one may have witnessed it fall, but there would have been something to see had someone been there. Not so with the resurrection. In the resurrection, Jesus passed through death to life. In their bearing witness to this passing, the disciples were claiming that the rest of us, here and now, can make the same passage, yet without physically dying. Paul speaks of our being "dead to sin" but "alive to God" (Rom 6:11). There is a newness of life which God has made available to men and women here and now. This new life is a down-payment, since our present existence is not the final stage of our creation as God's children, but only the beginning.

The death and resurrection of Jesus are not straightforward, self-explanatory moments. They call for interpretation. The report that Jesus died tells us very little. We need to know his story, the fateful steps which brought him to his death, in order to begin answering what his death on the cross meant. In the same way, the claim that Jesus was raised from the dead does not tell us very much. What does being raised from the dead mean? Why this violation of what nature intends for us, namely, our ultimate bodily dissolution? Death itself is not our enemy, since dying is a natural, even essential aspect of the creation which God pronounced good.

But if death is not our natural enemy, then the resurrection is not really aimed at destroying that death which is basically a fact of life. Far more crucially, the resurrection reveals the divine determination to reverse the conditions that kill human beings; it is a divine protest against violence and injustice, poverty and oppression, and everything else that enslaves human beings and their societies. Death becomes evil when it is primarily the denial of life and a frustration of the human spirit. The raising of Jesus from the dead is the Christian community's interpretive key for discerning God's action within human history.

Religious writers today remind us repeatedly that death and resurrection have to be taken together, for the one who was raised from the dead was the crucified Jesus of Nazareth. His being crucified thus defines or qualifies his being raised. In raising Jesus, God was doing more than calling him personally back to life, in the way, for instance, that Elisha called back the son of the Shunammite woman (2 Kgs 4), or Paul revived the young boy who had fallen from the window (Acts 20), or Jesus restored Jairus' daughter (Mk 5) and summoned Lazarus back (Jn 11). The death of Jesus conjures up for us the whole history of humanity oppressed and tortured, enslaved and impoverished. Thus the resurrection always has to be related to the larger human story and God's everlasting concern to rid creation of that kind of death and draw it along the way of justice. Paul would have called it the way of reconciliation (2 Cor 5:19).

The Resurrection and Paul

When we speak about Jesus' death, or when we proclaim "Dying you destroyed our death," it is not death in the abstract that we should have in mind, that final act of every human being's existence or that ultimate and unequivocal sign of human finitude. On the contrary,

Jesus' dying occurred under a specific set of social, political and religious circumstances. In fact, the death of each and every one of us is unique, occurring as it must under a specific set of circumstances. Paul may have obscured this point when he contrasted Christ and Adam:

> Therefore, just as sin came into the world through one man, and death came through sin, and so death spread to all because all have sinned…. (Rom 5:12)

> For if the many died through one man's trespass, much more surely have the grace of God and the free gift of the one man, Jesus Christ, abounded for the many. (5:15)

> Therefore just as one man's trespass led to condemnation for all, so one man's act of righteousness leads to justification and life for all. (5:18)

What seized Paul's attention here was not Jesus' death defined by the concrete circumstances related in the gospel, but a death which abstracts from history and which has taken on truly cosmic proportions. Even the cross, that most specific reminder of the particular political and religious conditions which ended the life of Jesus, is transformed into an apolitical symbol of suffering, surrender and humiliation. Thus the power of the cross, for Paul, is directed against sin as such and not just the particular historical form of sinfulness which brought Jesus to his death. The scandalous injustice which the cross represents gets lost in the ultimate victory over death in general.

In short, as a result of Paul's comparing Christ and Adam, all of us, no matter what the reasons for our individual deaths—cancer, old age, auto accidents, heart failure, and so on—can relate to the cross of Jesus, since in him *all* have died, and not just the martyrs for justice and the victims of slavery, poverty and oppression. The cross of Jesus no longer gives enduring form or expression to all the crucified men and women of history, but to every last one of us. Yet to lose sight of Jesus' dying as a death by crucifixion, however, is to miss what might be central in the message of his being raised from the dead. All human suffering, whatever its genesis, would thus be symbolically transformed by the cross of Jesus. No matter how inspiring or uplifting this sounds, the historical crucifixion of Jesus cannot justify a spirituality of suffering.[5] The message of the cross and resurrection reveals much more about solidarity than about suffering.

Resurrection, we have suggested, is an *interpretation* of what happened to Jesus; salvation was what the disciples actually experienced. Again, I think the clearest illustration of this is found in Paul. Although he was the earliest of the New Testament writers, our historical imagination may deceive us a little. The gospel narratives sound as if they antedate Paul, who actually came on the scene after Pentecost. After all, *first* came John the Baptist and the ministry of Jesus, *then* afterward the apostles and the early church. Furthermore, in the arrangement of New Testament writings, the gospels precede the letters of Paul.

Yet while the story of Jesus obviously unfolded before Paul's Christian career commenced, Paul wrote before any of the evangelists, and thus his account of having seen the risen Jesus precedes the Easter stories as recorded in the gospels. Paul was speaking and writing from within his experience of Jesus risen in a way that the evangelists either could not or chose not to do.[6]

Paul's experience was not, we should add, what he (or anyone else, for that matter) would have actually observed, if he had been waiting by the entrance to the tomb at sunrise on "the third day." On the part of Jesus' disciples, the very idea of Jesus being raised from the dead would have taken some time to get used to, to fathom and to connect with the rest of their experience. They would eventually search through the scriptures for assistance in making sense of what had happened to Jesus, a reflective process quite evident in many New Testament writings.

Paul, however, would have learned about Jesus through the early Christian movement, not through first-hand contact with Jesus in the days of his ministry. Paul obviously knew the claims being made by Jesus' followers that he had been raised from the dead. Therefore, Paul's encounter with Jesus risen would have been noticeably different from that of the others. Jesus raised from the dead was something Paul had heard about and at first would have rejected in principle; the early apostolic preaching must have offended his sensibilities terribly.

Easter certainly turned the disciples' world upside down, but in Paul's case it also turned that world inside out and completely reversed his whole way of thinking and believing (see Philippians 3:7–11). Paul would have brought to that encounter with the risen Jesus his particular strengths and weaknesses, his religious training and social background, and above all, perhaps, a yearning for deliverance shaped by the painful groping of his own mind and heart. Paul's encounter with the risen Jesus, we might say, would have been quite different from Peter's. What salvation therefore would have meant to each of them, at least initially, would also have been markedly different.

Now while Paul was radically transformed by his encounter with the risen Christ, the way he interpreted that experience by explaining who and what Christ was all about had the effect, as we have noted earlier, of removing Christ from his earthly history and elevating him to a cosmic or universal plane. The great figure with whom Paul constantly contrasted Christ was Adam. But Adam is not just a literary character in the book of Genesis; the figure of Adam is mythological. To parallel Christ with Adam, therefore, poses the danger of mythologizing Christ. The second Adam becomes the great champion of human salvation, while through the first Adam sin and death entered the world. The first Adam grasped for glory and grandeur; the second Adam embraced rejection and humiliation. And so on. The parallel is rich from the point of view of literary symbol; but it is theologically risky, because it tends to overlook the actual history of Jesus, even if we cannot be certain of many of the concrete details of Jesus' life.

The fact is, however, that Jesus had a history, and in our imagination he needs to be inserted within a history. The failure to root Jesus securely in this world would jeopardize human salvation *in its totality*. The corrective lens, fortunately, is provided by the gospel which proclaims the kingdom of God as the historical form of the divine promise. Not the next world; *this* one. Not the future life; *this* life. Not salvation from a figurative death; salvation from *real* death. That is, deliverance from the evils which kill men and women by stealing their humanity, even their very souls.

Paul undoubtedly experienced newness of life, or what the fourth gospel referred to as being reborn of the Spirit (Jn 3:5). Paul's was not the only possible form of such an experience, however. Other people could experience newness of life in terms of their particular situations, backgrounds and deeply personal needs. What salvation might have meant to Paul as he instructed various communities about the gospel which he believed Christ had entrusted to him need not be what it would mean for everyone. The fourth-century Christians who flocked to the desert of Egypt in search of perfection would not have conceived salvation the way a family living in a barrio in Manila or São

Paulo today would, or a middle-class couple in a North American suburb might. Paul does write, for example,

> I have been crucified with Christ; and it is no longer I who live, but it is Christ who lives in me. (Gal 2:19–20)

> May I never boast of anything except the cross of our Lord Jesus Christ, by which the world has been crucified to me, and I to the world. (Gal 6:14)

> I want to know Christ and the power of his resurrection and the sharing of his sufferings by becoming like him in his death....(Phil 3:10)

Paul does not actually tell us what being *crucified* with Christ means, or what being *crucified* to the world means, or what becoming *like Christ in his death* means. We can be sure that dying with Christ consisted of a symbolic passing from an old life of sin to a new life of grace through baptism (see Romans 6). But the historical form of Jesus' death was crucifixion. Presumably, then, a person who experiences himself *crucified* with Christ or becoming like Christ in the manner of his dying is interpreting *the way he now lives* in terms of the cross of Jesus.

But if being crucified is not merely a symbolic or poetic expression of a present experience of any kind of suffering human beings might endure; if being crucified with Christ implies being drawn into his mission on behalf of the kingdom of God and enduring the consequences; if being crucified with Christ means being "nailed" to the lives and fortunes of human beings poor and oppressed, then we have a way of reattaching Paul's language to history. The resurrection, therefore, brings to full expression divine solidarity with the world in its brokenness.

Yet there is something else to consider here. Just as the term "resurrection" is shorthand for an experience of liberation and newness of life, so also Paul's passionate phrase "crucified with Christ." For "crucified with Christ" is a dramatic and powerful description of salvation: Paul knows himself saved and liberated in his being united with the cross of Christ. Death and life come together here so closely that they cannot be pulled apart without doing violence to the underlying experience. The fourth gospel comes at the same point from a different angle. For John, the moment of humiliation and death is the moment of exaltation: "And I, when I am lifted up from the earth, will draw all people to myself" (Jn 12:32). In Paul's case we find someone leading a crucified existence, or an existence with the crucified one, and for the first time in his life really comprehending what being fully alive means.

Now, where does this leave us? What relevance does Paul's insight into leading a "crucified existence" hold for the way we think of resurrection and salvation today?

If we pursue Paul's line of thinking, then the Christ with whom he is being crucified is still being crucified, for Paul is not talking about the pre-Easter Jesus. Otherwise, his language would not make sense; he could not be crucified with Christ if that death were over and done with. The Christ of whom Paul speaks, therefore, must be the risen Christ, and the direction of Paul's language thus leads us to think that the passion of Christ is continuing in the world. Or perhaps more sharply, the passion of Christ continues in the suffering of men and women. But, as we already noted, the form of this suffering cannot be simply suffering in general; otherwise it loses its groundedness in the story of Jesus.

Secondly, Paul's language would lead one to think that the experience of being crucified with Christ and being liberated are two sides of the same coin. It is not as if Paul is saying, "*First* I was crucified with Christ, *then* I was liberated with Christ." The two moments may be conceptually distinct, but they could very well be referring to a rather complex religious experience. Paul feels himself more alive and liberated or set free precisely in the moment of his joining himself to Christ crucified. To transpose this idea we might say that Christians know themselves to be newly alive and set free at that moment when they are joined to the world which even now is undergoing crucifixion. A union of mind and heart with men and women who are victims of injustice may be the closest we can come to realizing the insight embedded in Paul's letters.

Perhaps now the connection between the resurrection and the desert through which we are passing has come into focus. It seems to me that there is no way we could sustain ourselves in the wilderness of the world's suffering unless we also discovered there the presence of God, who keeps our hope alive. For if there is nothing more to the world—and to life—than desert, then we shall all perish.

Is it not true to say that for Christians resurrection is the experience of wilderness transformed? Every victim of hunger and poverty, every child lost to genocide, every young girl forced into slavery in the sweat shops of the third world, every infant that dies for lack of clean water, every peasant murdered by death squads, every youngster orphaned by war or maimed by a landmine: the litany is virtually endless, yet each one of them could be one more flesh-and-blood argument against hope. Even if we have never had to meet the world's poor face to face, we should at least realize that they greatly outnumber us. We cannot shelter ourselves against them forever and still claim to be people of faith. Men and women who want to follow Jesus have no choice but to join them somehow; and that means abandoning our oasis and venturing into the desert. Or to switch metaphors, it might also mean joining a rebellion.

Drawing on his experience as a street lawyer and social activist in East Harlem, William Stringfellow wrote:

> *Resurrection is verified where rebellion against the demonic thrives....*I am not being romantic in using Harlem as symbol, particularly when I refer to Harlem in rebellion as signifying the resurrection. I am, however, affirming that in the black ghetto there is a resistance to death as social purpose, a perseverance in living as human beings, a transcendence of the demonic which is at least *an* image of resurrection which exposes and challenges the reign of death in this society and which, thus, benefits all human beings.[7]

But lest this sound as if Christian faith today is utterly joyless, I should add that our faith in Jesus risen is what remakes the desert. To say that he is risen means that he lives *somewhere*. The resurrection does not cancel out the hard, immovable reality of suffering, and it does not urge us simply to look beyond the world's pain and desperation. Rather, resurrection for us might well be the experience of knowing God in, with and among the poor and the expendable ones of contemporary society. *In them* because God has taken their side. *With them* because we cannot know God alone; we know him together, or not at all. *Among them* because God always walks with his chosen people. Paul spoke of power being made perfect in weakness (2 Cor 12:9); that was one of his ways of describing the saving experience we call the resurrection. We might choose to speak in terms of "hope being made perfect in the wilderness," and if hope, then love too. Resurrection is one way of describing a world remade. God is also there, and for that reason in our prayer we face the world without ever losing our moral and spiritual nerve. Paul believed that no one could genuinely profess, in word and deed, that Jesus was Lord, except in the Spirit (1 Cor 12:3). I would venture a paraphrase of Paul's text: If we did not believe in the resurrection, we would certainly pray very differently; in fact, we might not be praying at all.

8

Who Is In, Who Is Out: The Parable of the Vineyard

A major lesson of the Christian interior life is that fidelity to prayer universalizes our concerns. It is easy to understand why this should happen. If stepping into God's presence eventually leads into sharing what is of concern to God, then the natural movement of prayer is toward the experience of solidarity. To be with God is to be with the world which God created and loves, redeemed and accompanies. The activity of praying enlarges the scope of our desires. It also concretizes those desires by pulling us into the historical experience of our sisters and brothers, especially those on the bottom.

Development of the interior life is not unlike growth in the other areas of our lives. If human beings are growing and maturing, then it is quite likely that they are successfully working through the tensions, challenges and problems appropriate to their age, social and physical condition, and so forth. The maturing of faith and the development of prayer is neither smooth nor effortless, as most of us can testify. There may have been numerous occasions in which we have sensed ourselves being pulled apart, tested, frustrated and wrung dry without knowing why. The Spirit does not play games with us, of course; it instructs and makes strong. But learning to pray, or to walk prayerfully before God, is not always simple. In fact, the more serious we are about it, the more demanding prayer becomes.

The process by which we are pried open interiorly so that we become ever more open to God's action in the world and in our own lives typically includes moments of surprise, embarrassment and exasperation. In addition it normally involves coming face to face with the reality of sin in our lives, a realization made all the more humbling in light of God's goodness. But most of all the process involves discovering just how small and suffocating our private worlds can sometimes be. Even the aridity people occasionally mention in describing their interior life may be related to a slowness, even a failure, to develop a mind and heart really joined to the world.

It is important to be clear here. The world without God is going to feel like a spiritual wasteland, and God without the world is spiritually uninteresting and unsatisfying. In prayer, God and world must come together. Otherwise there is bound to be a dryness, emptiness and boredom which stifles all desire. Whenever people regularly attentive to the interior life complain that their prayer has become dry, an initial prudent response might be to inquire what has happened to their sense of the world. The inner purging or cleansing which has been classically associated with the development of the interior life might well be connected with the absence of the poor in our prayer. If the poor are not there, then the Spirit will start prying us open and burning away those things that have been keeping the poor out of our minds and hearts. There may be no other means of reversing the effects of spiritual erosion than fresh immersion into the world; that stripping away constitutes asceticism at its best—or worst, depending on one's point of view.

A similar dynamic may have been at work in the gospel story, particularly at those moments when Jesus began teaching in parables. Indeed, the parables might even be said to mirror what happens in the course of praying. And if the parables originated with Jesus, then they may also mirror some of the dynamics of his interior life, for Jesus would not have been able to teach convincingly what he had not first learned. The parables work our imaginations over, challenging us to look at God and the world with different eyes. They can serve as primers for prayer.

For people who like parables, the world is a potential gold mine. Countless stories, events, encounters and so on are just begging for modern-day evangelists to record them and give them religious shape. Everyday life contains more than enough material to write a thousand gospels, each one containing stories drawn from the activities and business of the little worlds we know so well, yet stories that are capable of catapulting the imagination into a much larger space. Adapt some of the landscape, costumes and professions, and the imagery which appears in Jesus' parables has its counterpart in our lives today.

A Short Word About the Parables

To say that Jesus' parables must have been thought-provoking would be understating things considerably. Not only do his parables tease reflections out of us (what on earth, we ask, was Jesus getting at?), but they also chip away at some of our most confident and comfortable assumptions (he could not mean *that*, could he?). After hearing the parable about the vineyard workers who all received the same wage, although some had begun laboring early in the morning while others had not started until late in the afternoon, we nearly stumble over the apparent lack of equity (Mt 20:1–16). Jesus could not possibly have meant what I think he was saying, could he? Is he telling us that the amount of time and sweat we put into our efforts to lead decent lives ultimately will not merit us a greater reward than those countless human beings who labored less? If so, doesn't this undermine the ethical foundation upon which our economic and social life is built where reward is commensurate with effort?

Consider, for instance, one of the best known parables. We hear the story about the man fallen among robbers, where the person who comes to the poor man's assistance is not a religious figure (the priest or the levite), but a godless Samaritan. Why, we ask, does Jesus cast the two individuals so intimately connected with worship service in such an unfavorable light, while giving the filthy Samaritan the starring role? Was Jesus suggesting that people with the reputation of being irreligious might be more sensitive to what is of God than those steeped in religious observance? Is he merely saying that compassion is what counts above everything else? Or is he challenging his hearers to examine their insider/outsider category so as to warn them that those people they esteem the least might be the very ones (and the only ones!) who are pleasing to God?

The parables would be far less interesting if they had only one application. Their richness arises from their implied universality. I can ask, for instance, who are the Samaritans in my life, or in my community, or in my social class, or in my country. If the neighbor is the person who needs my assistance here and now, then who is actually my neighbor: the family living next door, or a community across the city, or even people on the other side of the world?

A personal favorite is the parable about the old wine and the new wineskins. On the face of it, this text seems to be simply a way of getting us to realize that old, brittle categories cannot tolerate the strain of new ideas. If I am convinced, for example, that the world is flat or that it is fixed at the center of the universe, because that is what my eyes tell me and that is what everybody with a brain takes to be evident, then I might find it downright ludicrous, perhaps even blasphemous, when I hear some arguing the contrary against common sense, men of science and the revealed word of God itself!

But the reason why this parable bites has to do with what comes before it in the gospel narrative. The setting is a potentially embarrassing question posed to Jesus by the people as they compared the disciples of John the Baptist and the Pharisees with Jesus' followers. The text reads:

> Now John's disciples and the Pharisees were fasting; and people came and said to him, "Why do John's disciples and the disciples of the Pharisees fast, but your disciples do not fast?" Jesus said to them, "The wedding guests cannot fast while the bridegroom is with them, can they? As long as they have the bridegroom with them, they cannot fast. The days will come when the bridegroom is taken away from them, and then they will fast on that day." (Mk 2:18–20)

In order to appreciate this passage, we need to be aware that Jesus himself was not known for fasting the way other religious figures and groups would have been. The question makes better sense when we realize that the concern presented here was a challenge to the early church, not to Jesus himself.[1] Jesus would have been dead by this point; so too was John. The scene reflects a conflict between their respective followers. Perhaps the Christians felt somewhat threatened by the practice of certain devout Jews and the ascetically-minded disciples of John. *Real* spiritual people lead lives sharply marked by asceticism; they fast and pray regularly. One cannot imagine John the Baptist dancing and drinking at a wedding party; indeed, who would have invited him? But John was a *real* man of God; one knew he was a genuine prophet. After all, he even looked the part: camel hair, locusts, desert and all, someone straight from the bible's central casting. Likewise the Pharisees: they were absolutely serious about serving God, down to the last particular of the law. One could see at a glance that they were religious because they dressed and played the role perfectly. They knew which prayers to say on what occasions, they were scrupulous about keeping themselves ritually pure, and their piety was evident even in their garb. They fasted and gave alms as required; their lives were morally exemplary.

To a young Christian community still a little unsure of its place and identity, a few standard ascetical practices might prove advantageous. Since they could not ignore the fact that Jesus' behavior was markedly different from that of John and the Pharisees in this regard, the Christians may have resorted to inventing a saying of Jesus to justify the adoption of fasting "when the bridegroom is taken away."

Next there follow two sayings, one about not patching an old cloak with new cloth, and the other about wineskins:

> And no one puts new wine into old wineskins; other-
> wise, the wine will burst the skins, and the wine is
> lost, and so are the skins; but one puts new wine into
> fresh wineskins. (Mk 2:22)

The point is obvious. The fermenting process at work in the new wine would put too much of a strain on the old skins. The old skins are still useful; they serve a purpose. But they cannot tolerate the fermenting action of young wine.

Yet how are we to apply this saying? In its context, the saying appears to be Jesus' answer to the question about fasting. Jesus represents something new. His teaching, his way of being religious and expressing faith, marks a departure in some critical aspects from the customary and traditional. Jesus was not John, and he was not a Pharisee. Both of these figures represent something good, but the new thing which God was working in and through Jesus required new forms with which to receive and hold it. The older idea of what being holy, righteous and people of God meant, as incarnated by the disciples of the Pharisees and John, was preventing the people from acknowledging the Spirit's presence in Jesus.

Did Jesus mean, therefore, that people's notions of how God should behave could get in the way of their recognizing the action of God? Was he in effect calling for a thorough change of mind and heart—the new wineskins—in order to accept the revolutionary action of the Spirit? And to extend the point just a little, does the saying imply that what were new skins yesterday might be old skins tomorrow? In other words, do human beings constantly run the risk of approaching the mystery of God with frozen minds (to alter the metaphor), in which brittle ideas are so stuck to the mind's insides that to try pulling those ideas away could mortally wound a person's faith?

Jesus certainly never flaunted a new style of being religious; he was too humble and traditional for that. And for all the energy of his preaching there was nothing terribly revolutionary about his message; there was precious little in his preaching that could not be found somewhere in the scriptures. So why the problem? Apparently it was "people"—outsiders—who raised the question because they were perplexed about the behavior of Jesus' disciples. That behavior did not square with their preconceived notions. The reaction of the disciples, put on the defensive, is understandable.

Yet beneath all of that controversy there lay in the shadows another memory, another reality. It may be that

Jesus did not fast because the people with whom he largely associated could not do so. For all its discomfort, fasting remains a luxury of those who can afford not to eat, just as almsgiving is only possible to those who have some financial resources at their disposal. The poor are always fasting and their stomachs always ache, so when they have an opportunity to eat, even to indulge, they take advantage of it. The frequent references within the gospel to banquets and celebrating must surely be some indication of the hope which poor people entertained of someday having their fill.

In Jesus' own behavior, therefore, we do not have a willful violation of a cherished ascetical practice but a graced insight into the nature of God. The God of Israel was not pleased when the poor went hungry, and people would never realize this so long as their thinking was contained by the old skins. The only hunger which might have made sense to Jesus would have been the hunger pains resulting from sharing half of one's bread with the poor. The early church eventually took up periodic fasting as a way of expressing its intense longing for the return of Jesus: they began to fast when the bridegroom was taken away, and presumably they would end their fasting when he returned. The absence of Jesus was thus viewed as sufficient reason to go without food; the momentary ache of an empty stomach may have reminded them of his absence.

The new form—the new skin—which Jesus had been preaching about in his summons to "repent and believe" was the ability to view things from God's side, as it were. It may well be that Jesus was confronting the well-to-do, urging them to grasp reality from the underside of history; his teaching about wealth, obviously, was not directed to the destitute but to the rich. And it might also be that Jesus was attempting to get the poor (if we imagine the poor to have been the ones putting the question about his disciples' practice) to realize that fasting was hardly a necessary marker of holiness and being close to God. The piety of the poor and lowly can be easily preyed upon by religious experts. The experts, that is, the scribes, the teachers of the law, the educators, the directors of souls, provide instruction about the meaning and form of holiness, and on that score ordinary people could well feel left out, abandoned in the back of the synagogue.

But from God's side, there was no particular merit to fasting. Thomas Merton once remarked: "The norm of sacrifice is not the amount of pain it inflicts, but its power to break down walls of division, to heal wounds, to restore order and unity to the Body of Christ."[2] To paraphrase Merton, perhaps we could say that the norm of sacrifice is solidarity with communities of suffering. Ascetical practices which fail to increase our sense of oneness with them are not Christian. The gospel's "rich man" will not understand this until he opts to stand with the poor, and a poor person will not understand this so long as she is alienated from her own experience. In either case what is needed is fresh skins, fresh ways of looking at the world.

The Parable About the Wicked Tenants

We turn now to a text which is potentially scandalous, if not downright dangerous. It is a parable about divine repossession:

> "Listen to another parable. There was a landowner who planted a vineyard, put a fence around it, dug a wine press in it, and built a watchtower. Then he leased it to tenants and went to another country. When the harvest time had come, he sent his slaves to the tenants to collect his produce. But the tenants

seized his slaves and beat one, killed another, and stoned another. Again he sent other slaves, more than the first; and they treated them in the same way. Finally he sent his son to them, saying, 'They will respect my son.' But when the tenants saw the son, they said to themselves, 'This is the heir; come, let us kill him and get the inheritance.' So they seized him, threw him out of the vineyard, and killed him. Now when the owner of the vineyard comes, what will he do to those tenants?" They said to him, "He will put those wretches to a miserable death, and lease the vineyard to other tenants who will give him the produce at the harvest time."

And Jesus concluded:

"Therefore I tell you, the kingdom of God will be taken away from you and given to a people that produces the fruits of the kingdom." (Mt 21:33–41, 43)

It is not altogether certain whether this parable originated with Jesus, and, if it did come from him, what its initial form was. The parable envisions a social arrangement in which there are absentee landowners and tenant farmers, and if the parable had originally applied to *the situation in which Jesus lived*, then it is not impossible that its intention was strikingly different in its earlier form:

If at the earliest stage of the gospel tradition the story was not an allegory about God's dealings with Israel, as it is now, it may well have been a warning to landowners expropriating and exporting the produce of the land.[3]

In other words, Jesus may have been admonishing the wealthy landowners to deal justly with the poor, or else the tenants would take matters into their own hands! Initially, another scholar suggests, the vineyard owner may not have been a God-figure at all, but a rich man who took possession of fields that once belonged to poor peasants, a person who cared much more about getting his portion of the produce than the safety of the servants he sent to collect it. Rather than being tenants from hell, the peasants whose sweat and labor were spent on the vineyard were in effect desperately poor people mounting a revolt.[4]

In its present form, however, the meaning is sharp, but for a religious reason, not an economic or social one. God presumably is the ultimate "landowner" and the leaders of Israel would be the "tenants." The vineyard might then correspond to the people of God, while the wickedness of the tenants would refer to official religious mismanagement of God's people. Periodically, God sent prophets, only to have them abused and rejected by the leadership. Matthew makes the reference quite pointed: "When the chief priests and the Pharisees heard his parables, they realized he was speaking about them" (Mt 21:45). *The historical situation of the evangelist* was marked by a severe tension between the synagogue and the early church. The implication is that God has relieved the Jewish leadership of their charge and awarded oversight of the people of God to the church. Or perhaps even more bluntly, God has transferred the divine promise—the kingdom of God—to others, namely, to the Christian community as the faithful remnant of Israel.[5]

It is safe to assume that Matthew did not believe that a radical break had taken place between Israel and the church, for that would have been tantamount to a divine rejection of all the events of salvation history through which God had demonstrated his love and faithfulness to the Jewish people. There had to be continuity between Israel and the church if God was not to be charged with being capricious, inconsistent and untrustworthy. Yet what exactly did that continuity consist of, if God had taken away the vineyard and given it *to a people* that would produce the fruits of the kingdom? The vineyard, finally, did not stand for the people directly but the promise of the kingdom. The promise, therefore, was going to be *leased* to another people. Divine faithfulness evidently does not commit God to preserving the biological, cultural and historical identity of a particular race or nation, but to safeguarding the promise of the kingdom by entrusting it to those who would produce fruit for the harvest time.

While we may never learn what exactly Jesus intended to convey through this parable,[6] we can determine the purpose for which Matthew used it. He was not addressing the Jewish community, but the early church:

> While admitting that the previous tenants did not bear fruit, Matthew does not dwell on the rejection of the Jews but uses it as a warning to his own community....Matthew simultaneously warns his community that their status as tenants of God's vineyard should not be a source of presumption.[7]

Nevertheless, the very point Matthew draws here cannot be frozen in time. For if God was displeased with one set of tenant farmers, could he not become equally displeased with succeeding tenants, if fruit was not forthcoming, or if his messengers were treated so miserably? Might God, in other words, transfer the promise—the offer of the kingdom—to yet another people besides the new Israel which Matthew imagined? The very fact that Matthew incorporates such a warning in a document addressed to a Christian community would lead us to think that such a possibility should not automatically be ruled out.

Paul, it should be recalled, seems to have made a similar move. Righteousness before God comes from faith, not from physical descent, and certainly not from sheer observance of Israel's law. Paul writes:

> For the promise that he would inherit the world did not come to Abraham or to his descendants through the law but through the righteousness of faith. (Rom 4:13)

> For this reason it depends on faith, in order that the promise may rest on grace and be guaranteed to all his descendants, and not only to the adherents of the law but also to those who share the faith of Abraham (for he is the father of all of us, as it is written, "I have made you the father of many nations")—in the presence of the God in whom he believed....(4:16–17)

> For not all Israelites truly belong to Israel, and not all of Abraham's children are his true descendants....This means that it is not the children of the flesh who are the children of God, but the children of the promise are counted as descendants. (9:6–8)

Paul was making the case that the Gentiles had inherited the faith of Abraham and consequently deserved to be numbered among his descendants. Neither bloodlines, nor sacred traditions, nor divinely revealed ordinances, nor temple and cult, nor ethnicity could serve as the basis for being a true Israelite. Only faith, which was close to Matthew's "fruit" of repentance and conversion, qualified a person to be a member of God's chosen people. Paul had already witnessed the Gentiles responding to his gospel by repenting, converting and coming alive to the Spirit. That was all the proof he needed.

But back to the parable. Could Matthew really conceive the possibility that the promise would be taken away from the church and "leased" to "another nation," if Christians failed in the matter of discipleship? It would be hard to imagine Matthew agreeing with this prospect in light of Jesus' parting promise to be among his followers "to the end of the age" (Mt 28:20). Church and the risen Jesus belong together; how could one have Jesus (and discipleship) without the church? Only if the divine promise—the kingdom of God—were *independent* of Jesus and the church would it be possible to imagine its being offered to yet another people who would produce "fruits of the kingdom." The promise could not have been indissolubly wedded to Israel if, as the text reads, the vineyard can be leased out to others.

In short, Israel did not own the vineyard any more than the church could. The vineyard is divine property. Jesus announced the kingdom; he bore witness to the abiding promise of God. But if the vineyard belongs to God, then God can do whatever God wishes. Access to the kingdom is God's to give, and to take away. Corresponding to the kingdom and the promise are humanity's deepest, best hopes for a world fully redeemed, liberated and sanctified. God alone can meet and satisfy those hopes. We for our part never have the right to say, for example, "Here and no place else is the promise of God offered and fulfilled." In this sense, not even Jesus can restrict access to God's grace. There are numerous men and women who have found God without ever having put their faith in the gospel.

The parable is a powerful reminder of the sovereignty of God and a necessary admonition to those who would presume on some entitlement. As John the Baptist warned:

> Bear fruits worthy of repentance. Do not begin to say
> to yourselves, "We have Abraham as our ancestor; for

> I tell you, God is able from these stones to raise up children to Abraham." (Lk 3:8)

God can do whatever God wishes, even to entrusting the promise to other nations when the people initially chosen proves itself faithless. If the church succeeded Israel as the bearer of God's promise, is it possible that some other community would succeed the church if we Christians failed to deliver "fruits worthy of repentance" in due season? Could God entrust the offer of the kingdom to Buddhists, or to Muslims, or to a community yet to be formed? The parable of the vineyard workers is indeed sobering.

Yet suppose the vineyard does refer to the people in the sense of Isaiah 5:7:

> For the vineyard of the Lord of hosts is the house of Israel, and the people of Judah are his pleasant planting.

And suppose further that the vineyard refers not to *all* without distinction, but above all to the poor and the lowly, whose interests had been neglected by the religious leaders who knew that "he was speaking about them" (Mt 21:45). Suppose the key that unlocks this possible meaning has been given to us by the beatitude:

> Blessed are you who are poor,
> for yours is the kingdom of God.
> (Lk 6:20)

If the single qualification for being offered the kingdom is being poor, then we may be finally approaching that characteristic which truly makes one a "child of Abraham" and a member of the chosen nation. For Paul, being a descendant of Abraham was another way of describing a person of faith, and it was undoubtedly very important to Paul's sense of himself as a son of Israel that he could trace a connection between his new faith and the tradition of his ancestors.

But the nation of the poor is unlike any other. The sole eligibility requirement for being included within it has nothing to do with national boundaries, language, race, culture or even religion. The fact that one is poor is sufficient to qualify him or her for membership among that people. Furthermore, if *that* is the nation God has chosen to be his own, then access to the divine promise is contingent upon being numbered among those people. In short, the vineyard is for the sake of the poor. I am not suggesting that when Matthew has Jesus say

> Therefore I tell you, the kingdom of God will be taken
> away from you and given to a people that produces
> the fruits of the kingdom

he means the kingdom *will* be given to the poor. The kingdom *is already* theirs, and *only* theirs. The rest of us can enter it only by becoming a member of that people to whom the promise of God has been revealed, that is to say, through our solidarity with the poor, in the same way that the Gentiles had to be grafted on to the people of Israel (Rom 11:17). Being grafted is thus another way of speaking about solidarity.

The wickedness of the original tenants consisted of avarice and greed: they refused to give the owner his share of the produce, and when they thought they saw an opportunity for owning the vineyard outright, they resorted to violence and murder. The owner, however, has already made his decision: the vineyard will be entrusted to others. The story of the vineyard accomplishes all things parables are meant to. It surprises and upsets us by uncovering an attitude or preconception which needs to be challenged, yet it is not told in order to turn us away from salvation.

Think of the action of the parable on our imaginations as the action of the Spirit, or think of it as a prayer dynamic, and then the story becomes an invitation to grow. We do not give up praying when prayer becomes hard, any more than we would choose not to continue developing psychologically, affectively and socially when life becomes truly challenging. To hear the parable and respond, not to reject its message, is to continue to grow in solidarity with the world.

9

The Liberation of Spirituality

The West African theologian Lamin Sanneh was asked the following question during an interview:

Some have proposed that liberation of humanity from all forms of oppression can constitute the ground for dialogue between religious traditions. Do you find that authentically Christian or simply an example of the liberal penchant for embracing culturally accept-able causes?

To which he replied:

I have a question about anything that defines religion in terms of possibilities reachable by human effort. I put the question in the form of the story of Maximilian Kolbe, the Polish priest who died for another man in a Nazi concentration camp. I wonder whether Kolbe would say that religion for him was political liberation only, and that, instead of giving his food self-sacrifi-cially to his fellow inmates, he should have pro-claimed liberation as what "religion" demanded. The Gospel, for me, has much more nuance than that. It's much more than a rational thing that is approved by the wisdom of the age in the way socio-political libera-tion is today. That is an inadequate way of dealing with the full range of religious claims and the richness of religious life. But it seems increasingly the one that both liberal and conservative American Christians—although facing in quite different directions—are fixed on, and it is a reductionism that is turning away many thoughtful people from the church, as the statistics show.[1]

The concern expressed here crops up whenever people start to discuss the pros and cons of liberation theology. Is the theology of liberation simply a late twentieth-century rendition of the nineteenth-century social gospel? Does the great urgency with which many earnest people today are advancing the preferential option for the poor reduce the good news of Jesus to a socio-political message? And is the current emphasis on political and economic liberation of oppressed people turning many thoughtful, devout believers away from the church?

The last question would be difficult to answer. Did the fierce preaching of Amos and Hosea, or the denunciations of Jeremiah, turn the people of their times away from religion? Were some thoughtful and devout Jews who had come to hear John the Baptist offended by the fire in his words? Indeed, the gospel shows us Jesus coming to John's defense on this score when he asked the people:

> "What did you go out to the desert to look at? A reed shaken by the wind? What then did you go out to see? Someone dressed in soft robes? Look, those who put on fine clothing and live in luxury are in royal palaces. What then did you go out to see? A prophet?" (Lk 7:24–26)

The implication of Jesus' questions is that if people had gone to the desert to hear a prophet of Israel, and found themselves offended by what he had to say to them, then they had only themselves to blame. In other words, do not fault a prophet for speaking and behaving like a prophet, especially when the heat of his message begins to scorch your conscience. Certainly, those who made the effort to go and listen to John must have been thoughtful people!

Yet what about the other questions raised by the interview? Is the good news being reduced today to a sociopolitical agenda for worldwide economic reform? While I believe these questions have been handled soundly by several liberation theologians, it cannot be stated often or strongly enough that the Christian experience of God carries us directly into the lives of the poor.[2] In saying this, I do not mean that every Christian will be engaged by the poor in the same way or to the same degree. But a person today cannot escape the gospel's clear and persistent protest against the conditions responsible for poverty and injustice which have destroyed so many individuals, families and communities. Jesus' bold, prophetic defense of the expendables of his day continues to challenge us. Geographical distances are no longer a barrier to our being mindful of the global poor. Even if, in the interest of self-preservation, we push away those scrambling for safety aboard our economic vessel, we shall never escape the reality of an ocean full of desperate faces as far as the eye can see.

No one can plead, either, that Christianity is a two-tiered religion. We do not belong to a church in which the ordinary believers are on the lower level, while those especially chosen occupy the higher one. The gospel's call to be perfect cuts across all vocational choices. Whether we find ourselves in marriage, or religious life, or ordained ministry, or some other form of Christian living yet to be recognized, the gospel calls us all equally to a perfect following of Christ. The wider world is going to impinge upon all of us if in fact we are sincere about finding God in Jesus.

Since the very beginning of their history, Christians

have taken Jesus' lesson about loving and serving the neighbor with the utmost seriousness. Such love has been the touchstone of faith, for "faith by itself, if it has no works, is dead" (Jas 2:17). Furthermore, many disciples found it easier to love and serve those in need if they could see in their neighbor the features of Christ. To serve the least of Jesus' brothers and sisters was to serve Jesus himself (Mt 25:40). Nevertheless, to behold Jesus in others, especially the stranger in need, is one thing; to see the other as one's brother or sister in the most real and basic sense of the word is something else. Many of us have learned to "impose" Jesus on the features of other men and women; we have learned to serve *him* in others. But we may be much slower, even reticent, when it comes to recognizing those others as members of our family or ever admitting that we belong to theirs.

To arrive at this way of responding and relating to other human beings, our inner vision has to be converted and transformed. Such conversion and transformation is exactly what the preferential option for the poor is all about, and the preferential option is indeed something fresh, something distinctive about the situation of faith today. The great human virtue of compassion acquires a decidedly gospel slant when it is specified in the direction of the poor and oppressed. The words of the Peruvian theologian Gustavo Gutiérrez deserve to be weighed carefully:

> A response to the call of the poor requires that we pose ourselves a question in all honesty. How can we make faith in the God who "has a very fresh and living memory of the smallest and most forgotten" the inspiration of our lives? How can we transform this time of dissipation and death into a time of calling and grace? In other words, how can we make our own today the counsel the great apostle Paul received from

the "pillars" of the church—to be "mindful of the poor" (Gal 2:9–10)?[3]

There is no doubt that in the course of praying we can be motivated anew to act lovingly and justly, and the benefit of this should not be underestimated. But when the activity of praying flows from and leads back to an experience of solidarity with the world, we will never be lacking in motivation. Patience and hope might flag at times, but not our motive for acting at all times according to the gospel.

Spirituality Is Not an Escape

There have been times when growth in the interior life was measured in terms of self-denial and mortification, and the great pioneers of the way of the Spirit withdrew to caves and deserts. Many of them soon discovered, however, that no matter how far into the desert they journeyed or no matter how remote their monasteries, the "world" in the sense of fallen human nature always managed to track them down. They could not escape through prayer and spirituality any part of the human struggle. To the contrary, for those who embraced the life of prayer that struggle often appeared to become more intense.

If spirituality does not provide an escape either from the world or from the fallenness which afflicts every human being, neither does it provide a means of escaping the limitations of the church. As some people grow increasingly disappointed and disillusioned with the institutional church and its leadership, they take refuge in a remote interior cave where they can distance themselves religiously from the mass of their fellow Christians. Sometimes they create in their imaginations the ideal church or the ideal community. These constructions do not exist, of course, except in their minds.

Perhaps the sense of belonging inwardly to that ideal community, that is, to the church as the apostles supposedly envisioned it on Pentecost, provides a safety net for men and women disaffected with the institutional church. For them, the true church exists in the hearts of truly devoted disciples of Jesus. Nevertheless, while belonging to the church entails a spiritual communion with others, it also means being part of an historical community which is both visible and identifiable. One can understand why some Christians out of frustration would join a cult or a sect, while others might simply give up on finding a more perfect church and resign themselves to mediocrity. Or they might turn to a form of spirituality which is essentially elitist. Theirs would not exactly be the attitude of the Pharisee who prays, as the gospel points out, *standing by himself*, "God, I thank you that I am not like other people" (Lk 18:11). These people are not hypocrites who refuse to recognize their need for mercy and grace, but they do set themselves apart in that interior space where their spirit meets God's Spirit. Standing apart, they ultimately make things worse for the church and weaken corporate efforts to bring about greater solidarity with men and women in distress.[4]

It stands to reason, of course, that some Christians are going to have a keener grasp of their faith than others. They spend more time studying and praying, thinking and questioning, renewing themselves and worshiping with others. They may have a more acute sense of the ways of the Spirit; that is, they know how to discern, how to sift through their feelings, desires, thoughts and choices in order to find their heart's true center. Christianity, like the other major religious traditions, has a long history of men and women who have really known God and can assist others in their spiritual development.

Yet however expert those religious figures have been, a major feature of their lives is that ordinarily they never cut themselves off from the rest of the people of God, no matter how sorry the state of popular belief or how dismal the condition of popular practice. They might, as in the case of the Protestant reformers, establish a counter-church; or they might, in the interest of both serving and renewing the universal church, found religious congregations. But they do not retreat to "a church within the church." The elitism of that mentality offends genuinely Christian sensibilities and would lead us to question the soundness of a person's insight into the gospel. The idea of a spiritual "in-group" runs contrary to the basic equality we enjoy before God as a result of our common baptism.

Did Jesus Have a Privileged Experience of God?

The answer to this question appears so obvious, why would anyone ever bother to raise it? Doesn't the gospel tell us that God spoke to Jesus at key moments, such as his baptism and the transfiguration? And does it not seem logical that God would have communicated directly and immediately with Jesus during those times when he went apart and prayed? The divine voice-over in these scenes, which was actually the voice of the evangelists, referred to Jesus as "my Son, the Beloved" (Mk 1:11) and "my Son, my Chosen" (Lk 9:35). If Jesus is Son, then God must be Father.

Theologians have commented at length on the significance of Jesus' "*Abba* experience." The word *Abba* implies intimacy and tender familiarity. Therefore, according to some religious writers, Jesus' choice of that word to address God indirectly tells us about the depth of his relationship with God, his unbounded confidence in God, and his sense of being especially beloved.[5] Therefore, what is the point of the question?

There are at least two reasons for asking it. First, the idea that one's religious experience has a right to be privileged simply because it is mine or yours often functions in the spiritual life the way that the appeal to conscience sometimes operates in the moral life. It can lead to a pernicious individualism. That is not to suggest we should be afraid of our experience, but if it should happen that a person's religious life begins to isolate him or her from the wider communion of Jesus' followers, then some intuition has almost certainly gone haywire.

Indeed, our consciences are sacred. However, while safeguarding the integrity of individual liberty, we should not lose sight of the fact that to be human is to live and to grow in relationship with other men and women. This truth applies the brakes to any premature appeal to one's own experience along the lines of "God has spoken to me" or "I have prayed about such and such, and therefore..." or "I think the Lord is asking me...." This way of speaking is unfortunate. It suggests that God communicates secret messages to those who pray and that we pray in order to be able to hear those secrets.

What often justifies the idea, at least in part, that in prayer God is actually revealing to us what we are supposed to do and think is the unspoken assumption that God communicated directly with Jesus in his prayer. Jesus' actions and teaching were grounded, the supposition runs, in an experience of God which was fundamental to his self-understanding and which justified everything he did. And if that is the way things were with Jesus, the model of a true believer, then naturally it should be that way with us as well. The quintessentially Christian experience thereby becomes intimacy with God.

One place where this misapprehension shows itself is in the tendency to interpret biblical texts too self-referentially, as we have already seen. A reader applies the great call texts, such as that in Jeremiah 1:5, directly to his or her own life:

> Before I formed you in the womb I knew you,
> and before you were born I consecrated you;
> I appointed you a prophet to the nations.

And why not? The passage reflects a profound, consoling experience of being seized by God for some mysterious divine plan. Is that not what God did in the case of Jesus, the "model believer"? And would not that experience have served as the empowering source of his mission? The individuals who are probably more likely to appropriate such passages are priests and religious; such dramatic, prophetic calling does not seem to encompass ordinary Christians but only the exceptional ones among us.

The difficulty here is not that people claim to have rich religious inner moments; we obviously do. Rather, the difficulty is that unless those moments are in principle available to all of God's people, our religion runs the risk of becoming exclusionist and two-tiered, composed of those who have been granted the experience and those who have not. Moreover, when the gospel portrait of Jesus is pressed into service in this matter, then either all of us are outsiders and he alone belongs to God's inner circle, or else Jesus and some of his closest followers share that circle while the rest of us must content ourselves with the instruction they impart to us.

The second reason for wondering whether Jesus actually had a privileged experience of God is that it forces us to reflect on where such experiences might conceivably come from. Any suggestion that somehow God "infuses" knowledge and insight into us betrays a mistaken sense of how human beings have been created. Without our bodily senses and imagination we would be absolutely stuck, and no divine word could ever get through.

Our experience of God, therefore, cannot be dissociated from the world around us, from other people, and from the many stories, traditions, memories and lessons which make up our collective history. What takes place in so-called "privileged" experience is not that some new truth or possibility is poured into us from the heavens, but that some aspect of a person's experience is intensified enormously. In that "intensification of experience" the person does not see all of reality, but he or she does catch a segment of reality with such clarity and energy that the person's whole way of looking at the world is radically altered. We might even say that as a result a "new reality" has been created.[6]

In the case of Jesus, perhaps that new reality was the kingdom of God. The phrase itself has strong biblical roots, but Jesus gave it a fresh definition. And how did he do that? Here I am guessing, but assuming that we are on the right track so far, then maybe the answer lies in an intensification of his experience, a concentration of his vision. What actually was being intensified in his heart and mind, however, was the experience of the men and women around him, particularly those heavily burdened under the yoke of poverty and injustice, and who longed for salvation and deliverance. Jesus connected their experience—the stories which made up their lives: their struggles to repay debts, or to pay taxes, or to hold on to their parcels of land, or to find food for their families—with the holy mystery of God. The kingdom of God was what had seized him and the gospel proclamation was what resulted.

In the end, therefore, did Jesus enjoy a privileged experience of God? If that were to mean a miraculous revelation from the outside or from the heavens which was exclusively his and inaccessible to everyone else, then the answer ought to be no. But if we understand, first, that experience arises from our engagement with the world around us, and, secondly, that God encounters us in and through that experience, and if by "privileged" we mean "special," "distinctive" and "intense," the answer ought to be yes. What we have in Jesus' preaching the kingdom of God is an intensification within himself of *other people's experience*. Jesus had felt *their lives* with a holy passion, reminiscent of the great prophets of Israel. Hence the compassion, the zeal, the anger, the fidelity and the hope which characterized his preaching.[7]

The idea that I have just sketched is hardly new; it is simply another way to describe how revelation happens.[8] But this old idea gets a new twist when we suggest that the preferential option for the poor represents an intensification of our experience. With particular intensity and feeling we enter their world, trusting in the power of God to save and transform all of us. The consequence of that entrance is solidarity with the poor in a way that is neither naive nor romantic. We may never be able to see clearly all the implications of that solidarity, or what challenges and heartaches it may pull us into. We cannot physically swap places with the poor, and most of us are not in a position to live and raise our families among them. Ghettos, housing projects and inner cities can be dangerous, unhealthy places. Nevertheless, in loyalty and affection, in political and economic orientation, in our ethical sensibilities and worship, we will be increasingly and irreversibly mindful of them.

Yet what about the so-called *"Abba* experience" of Jesus? Here I would suggest that we have to be careful not to read too much significance into it. That Jesus knew God is abundantly evident throughout the entire gospel. None of his preaching about the kingdom of God, none of his parables and his healings, would make much sense if he had not experienced the God of Israel deeply and closely. And the word *Abba* connotes great filial trust and knowledge. But was such intimacy exclusive to Jesus?

It would be difficult to prove that no one in Israel had ever experienced God the same way prior to Jesus, although it seems very clear on the basis of the text from Paul's letter to the Romans

> …but you have received a spirit of adoption. When we cry, "Abba! Father!" it is that very spirit bearing witness with our spirit that we are children of God (8:15–16)

that as a result of being with Jesus his followers claimed to experience God the same way, namely, as daughters and as sons. The God who adopted the people of Israel and called them "son" (see Ex 4:22–23) has also adopted us. In this sense, therefore, Jesus' relationship to God was not exclusive. Indeed, *it would be impossible to prove that Jesus believed that he enjoyed a relationship with God that was qualitatively higher than that of his followers.*

But the major reason for not speculating too much on the nature of Jesus' *Abba* experience is that such speculation distracts us from what was truly central in Jesus' ministry, namely, the action of God in this world. As a result of over-speculating on God as *Abba*, we wind up concentrating excessively on Jesus' own person and identity, about which Jesus himself does not appear to have been preoccupied. Moreover, presenting Jesus in a way that highlights the unique character of his religious experience is not going to help us pray better. Jesus' experience of God is not authoritative because it was unique to him. While the truthfulness of Christian revelation certainly takes us back to the faith of Jesus, since he was in every sense of the word a believer, the faith of Jesus was also the faith of the people of Israel. Jesus' experience of God becomes authoritative at the point where we too come to share it and can say *on the basis of our own experience* that God is *Abba* for us as well.[9]

From What Does Spirituality Need To Be Set Free?

Christian spirituality today has become vulnerable to a number of misconceptions. One of the major ones is the idea that the reason for fostering the interior life and the goal of spirituality itself is peace of mind, equanimity, mystical oneness with the universe (or with the Absolute), inner bliss, moral perfection, or the heights of contemplation. However desirable these things may be in their own right, for Christian spirituality they can never be more than accompaniments in the course of one's basic search for God and they certainly should not define our ultimate goal for this life. The story of Jesus itself confirms the point. His life ends on the cross, and the last words Jesus utters, at least in Mark's account, are a cry—indeed, a *prayer*—of abandonment (Mk 15:34). That prayer sounds more like an experience of spiritual disaster than mystical union.

A second misconception occurs whenever people overlook the historical and the everyday in favor of the timeless and the universal. Christian spirituality in our time is being liberated from an excessive concentration upon the afterlife as a consequence of a more balanced approach to the resurrection. The raising of Jesus from the dead, we have realized, cannot be understood in isolation from his ministry and mission. Rather than turning our eyes away from this world toward the clouds, the resurrection directs us back to daily life with renewed hope and faith.

After recalling that history is the arena in which God's redemptive love unfolds, one British theologian asked:

> ...how could a whole tradition overlook the reality of the historical? It is not hard at all; indeed, the Christian tradition, despite its rootedness in historical testimony rather than in claims to authoritative experience, might well be said to have overlooked it for centuries! Human speculation seems to be naturally attracted to the timeless and changeless in its quest for ultimate explanation. Much in contemplative spiritual experience, too, seems to lead beyond the conditions of time and space to an ineffable Reality that cannot be limited by them. Does the doctrine of creation itself not suggest that the creator of time must be beyond time? In fact human spirituality almost inevitably moves to the idea of the Timeless, as it explores the limits of human experience and speculation. It is only the obstinate insistence that God has acted decisively for human salvation in Jesus that places an obstacle in the way of this natural theological propensity.[10]

For a Christian, the timeless and the universal are more than contemplative distractions; they are potential spiritual traps. And here the example of men and women renouncing the world and fleeing to the wilderness or to monasteries needs to be scrutinized carefully, lest we mistakenly conclude that a lifelong, full-time pursuit of the interior life is consistent with the gospel. Christians might indeed withdraw from their society, but one never abandons the world, because we always carry the world within us. Without the world we would have no soul; there would be no struggle, no temptation, no growth, no need for redemption.[11]

We ought to be grateful that some Christians have withdrawn into solitude to learn the ways of the human heart, for the lessons they learn illuminate and instruct the rest of us. But solitude without solidarity is not Christian. The God discovered on real or figurative mountaintops will have little to say to followers of Jesus. We must not idealize or romanticize such peak moments and experiences; otherwise we shall introduce an unnecessary tension into our religious lives. Forced to live in the everyday world, our minds and imaginations will be longing for that place apart where God is *truly* known, in the stillness and timelessness of the mountain and the desert, the forest and the endlessly pounding surf. The attraction to such places is strong, and as long as it holds sway, many are going to feel themselves spiritually second-class citizens, since they have no way of retreating from the world.

If preoccupation with the timeless creates a spiritual problem, so does the tendency to universalize. We believe that God's salvation has come to us in and through the gospel, but this belief does not mean automatically that Jesus has to be the universal savior. There are as many views of salvation as there are conditions from which men and women seek deliverance. Jesus did not address himself to *all* those needs, and thus he should not be made into a spiritual master key that will unlock every religious door in the world. By universalizing Jesus in our teaching and preaching we risk proclaiming someone who is no one's savior, because the story of Jesus unfolded in a particular time and place, under a particular set of social and economic needs.

Whenever the church stresses the universal mission of Jesus, it may be sacrificing the particular and concrete mission which began by the Jordan with the preaching of John.

The cosmos may have been redeemed and all hostile powers in heaven, on earth and under the earth may have been tamed, but what about human history? Might it not be wiser to start with historical forms of God's saving action and to recall that the "new heavens and the new earth" come from a vision of Christian hope for a world transformed? In short, both as an historical figure and as a symbol Jesus is not everybody's savior without differentiation. Above all, Jesus is savior for the poor and oppressed. His attention to those who had riches and power should be accounted for in terms of his underlying concern for those on the bottom. If the mighty ones repented, then the poor would be the beneficiaries of their conversion. Jesus was not a universal savior energetically trying to get everyone into heaven, but a prophet-like figure who believed with Isaiah that the good news of God was for the poor: good news, because it spelled their liberation.

A third misconception is that God encourages us to undertake penitential practices as a way of purifying our souls, as if bodily mortification in and of itself were a precondition for union with God. There is sufficient interior cleansing or purification of soul involved in our efforts to be faithful to what the Spirit asks of us day by day through the gospel without having to take on artificial suffering. And if it should happen that our own lives are fairly comfortable and our practice of the faith effortless, then we have only to look around us to the suffering and pain endured by so many others. The neighbor in need stands as a constant reminder of the gospel's demands.

There are cultures which are both poor and Christian where communities act out the passion story during Holy Week, complete with real scourging, real thorns and real nailing. But wherever there is actual, systemic poverty, people are already wearing a crown of thorns. The vivid enactment of the passion of Jesus mirrors what has been going on daily among the people, yet they have not been made reflectively aware of it. The sad outcome is that poor communities have frequently been alienated from their own experience and have been unable to recognize just how literally the story of Jesus has been their story too.

The connection between the two stories does not arise from the mere fact of suffering, but from suffering for similar reasons or under parallel circumstances. Whenever people engage in penitential practices *in the name of religion*, whether in the dramatic pageantry of a way of the cross or in self-inflicted pain, they imperil the understanding of God contained in the story of Jesus. The gospel does not summon the poor to take on their shoulders additional suffering, and the discipline to which the gospel calls the rich has nothing to do with private asceticism and everything to do with lifting burdens off the backs of their poor sisters and brothers. After all, is that not what God does:

> For the yoke of their burden,
>   and the bar across their shoulders,
>   the rod of their oppressor,
>   you have broken as on the day of Midian.
>   (Is 9:4)

I mention this because the cult of suffering lingers among us, less from a desire to inflict pain on ourselves than from an implied correlation between God and sacrifice. God, according to much religious rhetoric, appears to delight in sacrifice. Thus the more that we sacrifice, the closer we must be drawing to God. Some people find that, when life becomes thoroughly miserable and oppressive, it is comforting to take a long, meditative look at a crucifix and be reassured by the fact that Christ also suffered. However, it is one thing to discover in the cross a source of strength and another thing to believe that suffering is pleasing to God. The rhetoric of Jesus being "obedient to the point of death" (Phil 2:8) misleads us if we hear in those words a call to embrace suffering gladly because then we are imitating Christ.

An Unfinished Liberation

Some difficulties remain, however. Spirituality today still needs to be liberated from stereotypes about what holiness means and who exemplifies Christian holiness the best. I am not suggesting that we should cease honoring the great saints who have appeared among us over the centuries, or that there is something deficient in the traditional teaching that the fundamental determinant of Christian holiness is always charity, as Vatican II reminded us:

> Thus it is evident to everyone that all the faithful of Christ of whatever rank or status are called to the fullness of the Christian life and to the perfection of charity.[12]

Unfortunately, however, some of the models proposed to us for our edification and emulation have stood in the way of our becoming fully adult Christians.

Perfection is a tricky word. The gospel calls us to be perfect, as our heavenly Father is perfect (Mt 5:48). God's perfection, however, presents itself in terms of an unconditional love for every one of us, whatever our moral or spiritual state. God sends rain on the righteous and the unrighteous alike, as the gospel puts it. In the same way, we have been "called" to love our enemies and do good to those who hate us. Or since the premier divine quality is compassion, we must be as compassionate as God.

But whenever perfection is measured in terms of being consummately patient, or long-suffering, or being unable to refuse a request of any sort or from anyone, whenever perfection is presented to us in ways that exaggerate one particular feature or one special virtue of a person's life, faith is done a disservice. One saint might have been exemplary for humility, another for obedience, another for remaining steadfast under cruel persecution, another for severe mortification, or service to the sick, or for remaining chaste. Most of us, however, do not live with such concentration on one virtue. In our daily living we try to incorporate the spirit of the whole gospel, and at the end of each day we examine our consciences accordingly.

The point here is not that the majority of Christians are downright incapable of being perfect, even with respect to their favorite virtue; for we are indeed capable. Rather, the point is that holiness is often presented ideologically, as favoring and advocating one expression of Christian living over another. Priests and religious, for example, as men and women who renounced families and material goods have figured prominently in the roles of those declared saints and urged on us as examples of piety and faith. Unswerving loyalty to the authority of the church is praised, while courageous dissent and prophetic critique usually are not.

The models of holiness we need today are going to be provided for us by those men and women who have steeped themselves in the intricacies and the messiness of modern life, men and women who are no stranger to the often stressful business of grass roots neighborhood organizations, school committees, lobbying efforts on behalf of justice and peace, volunteer programs and so forth. These models will come from virtually all walks of life and largely from people with families to raise. Juggling time and energy, reaching for that balance which properly proportions the competing demands on their financial, emotional, physical, mental and spiritual resources, will require self-knowledge, prudence, and a faith community where belief is celebrated, nurtured and challenged.

Such Christians know that they must make a living within a political and economic system which constantly needs correction, reform and renewal. They will feel torn and compromised sometimes, caught between concrete responsibilities to their families and local communities, and a vision of the social world premised on justice and mercy. Those who live in western democratic societies face challenges to faith and belief which are historically and culturally distinctive. The form of holiness appropriate to men and women of our culture and our historical period is still being fleshed out by individuals who are trying as best they can in a complex age to live the gospel as they have come to understand it.

Above all, the central gospel virtues of compassion and love of enemies will need to be translated into a different idiom if we are going to catch their radical intent. When love of enemies is translated so as to mean love of the immigrant, the one who threatens my job security, or our national prosperity, who would put a heavy strain on our health care system, or our welfare programs; when compassion is translated to mean recognizing family likenesses in the faces of those staring at us each day from remote corners of the globe, desperate, terrified, famished: then we are grasping the gospel's cutting edge. Then, too, we may be on the way to formulating a definition of holiness appropriate to our time and place.

Finally, spirituality today may need to be liberated from an exaggeration of the role of spiritual directors. Several years ago the British writer Kenneth Leech observed:

> I am worried...that spiritual direction is being seen as
> more important than it is. It is, after all, one ministry
> among others....I detect now a tendency in some
> quarters to make the spiritual director more impor-
> tant than he or she is, in a way which is at variance
> with the mainstream of Christian tradition.[13]

Every one of us has an "interior life," although we
might lead it with greater or lesser degrees of attentiveness to
the presence of God. By virtue of our common baptism, and
maybe even more basically by virtue of our common humanity, we all share the universal call to holiness. For the one
Spirit which each of us has been given through baptism also
resides in each human heart as the mysterious source of
every life giving desire. The conviction that *all* are called to be
holy and to walk blamelessly before God has been gaining
ground steadily. It has forced us to rethink our traditional
understanding of religious vocation and priesthood, and to
develop a broader, more inclusive understanding of ministry,
together with a richer view of marriage and family life.

Nevertheless, the resurgence of interest in spirituality
which flowed from the conciliar vision of Christian holiness
has also yielded a new ministerial class, namely, the profes-
sionally trained spiritual director. The church sorely needs
men and women who have been schooled in the ways of
prayer and who can assist the rest of us as we seek clarity for
the decisions we need to make, or as we endeavor to grow in
faith and service. At the same time, however, we also ought
to avoid catering to the spiritual inferiority complex which
many of us have acquired over the years. I may envy an ath-
lete his prowess and skill, her agility and stamina; I may
envy a television celebrity's wit and good looks. I may
secretly admire those lucky few who have managed to make
millions of dollars, and I may admire people for their learning, their self-confidence, their ability to express themselves.

In fact, in their presence, I may feel a little intimidated by such accomplishments. Will I then carry that same sense of inadequacy and feeling second-best into my spiritual life? And will the belief that my humble experience and feeble insight simply do not measure up to the spiritual agility of the religious experts cause me to think and behave like a second-class Christian?

Spiritual insecurity must not be allowed to generate a new "expert" class of men and women who "know" about the things of God. In other words, we should not yield that sort of authority to others. Christian prayer, after all, is not an esoteric activity. A spiritual counselor or director, or a wise friend, can greatly help us in those times when we are attempting to sort things out, or when we need to ventilate our feelings and worries. But it is unlikely that the person is going to help us pray *better* if we have already been fairly earnest about the way we approach God. Spiritual dependency is not healthy for an adult Christian. Besides, numerous men and women have developed extraordinarily rich interior lives without ever having made a retreat or spent time under spiritual direction.

In the church, absolutely no one brokers access to the divine. No one has that right, that commission from the Lord, or that corner on the gospel. It would be a mistake if, having transcended the idea of the hierarchy as a priestly class (because of their association with the sacred) in favor of a renewed theology of baptism, we erected a new religious elite. The danger here is minimalized to the degree that we learn to discern and respect our own experience. And the threat is also reduced when spiritual directors themselves are imbued with the humility and honesty which comes from their own particular solidarity with the poor and oppressed. Those teach best who empower others to keep learning on their own.

10

The World as a School for Prayer

None of us prays in exactly the same way, nor are we expected to. We may share the same devotional practices, recite traditional prayers like the Our Father or Hail Mary, meditate on the same scriptures, attend the same eucharistic liturgy. Yet even then we do not pray alike. It is not just that the words themselves strike us differently, depending upon the state of our minds at a given moment. Rather, there are shades of difference in our images and notions of God and Jesus, in the thoroughness with which faith has imbued the way we look at the world, in the intensity of our love and compassion, in our personalities, our needs, and our religious and social sensibilities. These and numerous differences like them play important roles in how, when and where we pray.

Sometimes we pray with words, other times praying is wordless, even imageless. Sometimes prayer is a matter of being known by God, other times it is a matter of intense desire. For some people, praying takes form in their action, their work, their service, their deeds of compassion, or their love. Sometimes prayer is conscious, other times it is no more than an unconscious yet living relatedness to God. Sometimes prayer takes the form of an attitude or orientation, and other times its basic form is solidarity with the world. Praying, in other words, does not always consist of deliberately directing one's thoughts to God; there is more than one way to define it.

Praying is something that believers do as habitually as eating, sleeping or caring for their children. I do not mean that our families do not have to teach us about God and introduce us to the church; nor do I mean that we cannot learn, as we mature in our faith, various ways of enhancing our prayer. But praying is an activity which comes to us so naturally because we are made for conversation. We converse with people around us. We converse with ourselves in the solitude of our thoughts. And we converse with the world, that vast and nameless "other" which listens to our thoughts, before which we feel called upon to justify our behavior and give an accounting of our lives. Sometimes we even personalize the world, like children who see human forms in the configuration of puddles, spills, shadows cast by trees, or "faces in the clouds."[1] To personalize the heavens and the earth is to bring the world close, and that itself can be a prayerful moment.

At any rate, because we cannot exist without conversing, we are going to pray, whether people use that word or not. I am not attempting to prove this claim philosophically and I have not polled the world to test it sociologically. I am merely describing what I have observed about myself and others.

Prayer does not remain at the level of an amorphous conversation with life, however. For us as religious people, prayer turns into a basic posture we assume toward the world. Indeed, prayer could even be described as the way we face life; it is an expression of outlook and attitude, the obverse side of which is faith. As we have seen, prayer often goes beyond words and images to embrace actions and gestures. This is obviously the case with liturgical prayer, since liturgy abounds with symbolic gestures like the raising of hands, bowing of heads, tracing oneself with the sign of the cross, exchanging greetings of peace, standing and kneeling, and so forth.

In addition to liturgical gestures, however, there is the day-to-day action of working, serving, enabling, holding, loving and caring, listening, healing, feeding and clothing. The Christian prays through the whole of his or her life in ways that are often unconscious, for we do not have to be consciously attending to God in order to be praying. If we allowed ourselves adequate time to reflect, we might be surprised to discover how pervasive God's presence in our lives actually is. Everything about us reveals a deep, unassuming relatedness to the silent mystery of God. Someone observing how Christians live would see what prayer in action looks like.

Ordinarily, the activity of praying does not create any problem for us until we start to analyze what we do when we pray, or until we sense some dissatisfaction with the state of our relationship to God. We hear a talk, listen to a sermon, read a book or make a retreat, and some particular point may lead us to double back on what we do when we speak to God. That speaking then begins to strike us as forced, unreal, even silly. This sort of uneasiness typically does not last, however. Praying, like breathing, cannot remain interrupted for very long. Eventually it returns to its normal rhythm.

The second disturbance is the more crucial one. Being dissatisfied with one's relationship to God can lead a person to scrutinize the quality and depth of his or her life, and look for ways to improve it. There is no telling where those ways might take us, but one thing is certain. Praying is more than a matter of words, formulas, methods and techniques; it is more than a matter of frequency, duration, physical setting and bodily position. The best instruction Jesus left his followers about praying was his example: not his deportment while praying in the synagogue on the sabbath, nor his observance of religious festivals, nor his occasional forays to "deserted places" or mountaintops, because all these were the interval moments; but his actions, his zeal, his compassion and courage, his fidelity to the kingdom, his hope, his passion for justice and his solidarity with the people, because all of these revealed his posture toward the world.

There may be a certain awkwardness in trying to explain to someone in detail what we do when we pray, for there is something very intimate about praying. In the gospel scene where the disciples asked Jesus to teach them to pray (Lk 11:1), Jesus gave them what we call "the *Lord's* prayer," a designation which distinguishes that prayer from one composed by a saint, a rabbi, John the Baptist, or anybody else. No doubt, the evangelist designed that scene; Luke had his own reasons for emphasizing the role of prayer in a believer's life and for presenting Jesus as the great example of a person of prayer. To what extent Luke's emphasis corresponded with the historical figure of Jesus is hard to determine. Nevertheless, we can imagine the disciples speaking with Jesus on some occasion about prayer. The topic could have come up naturally and comfortably; after all, it comes up among us. We shall never know whether Jesus was conscious of the disciples' watching him while he prayed, or whether he may have offered the crowds some practical advice on how to deepen their attentiveness to God. To judge from the gospel accounts, Jesus had not presented himself as a grand master of prayer. The fact that the disciples requested a prayer suggests that it had not exactly occurred to Jesus to teach his disciples about praying in the way John had instructed those who followed him.

But when people ask for guidance with their prayer, they are seldom looking for fixed words to recite. Initially, they may be looking for reliable methods. In the *Spiritual Exercises*, for example, Ignatius Loyola offered three methods for those seeking to develop their prayer. The second and third methods propose various ways of walking through the Our Father. The second way involves meditating on each word of the prayer, while the third consists of "a measured rhythmical recitation."[2] Sometimes people need help getting started, and just as all of us at one time most likely relied on others to improve our reading skills, so also we may have to depend on others when, as novices to the interior life, we need guidance and insight to keep going forward.

Yet the solution to more satisfying prayer does not depend upon experimenting with different techniques. Whenever prayer is presented as something which can be facilitated by the proper technique or as a piously motivated mental exercise, the mind is likely to weary of it, the same way the body tires from a vigorous workout. After all, for many people exercise is simply the necessary means to fitness. Praying, however, should not be thought of as a "spiritual exercise" since it is less a means to an end than an expression of what we are inwardly as children of God.

If, as we have said, prayer is something we do more or less naturally, then the reason for the problems people frequently encounter might have a lot to do with the way prayer has been defined. The more restrictive the definition, the greater the likelihood that individuals will feel either guilty or dissatisfied when their prayer does not match up to what is expected. In general, the standard difficulties people recount include distractions, resistance to setting aside a fixed time for praying, impatience over meager results, a sense of wasting time. But are such things automatically symptomatic of a failure on our part, or a lack of expertise, or unrealistic expectations? Have we been instructed that prayer consists of an intense union with God, an experience of being loved and accepted, and as a result do we measure success or failure in prayer against whether we have been granted such an experience?

I would not dispute for a minute that many people in their prayer have experienced forgiveness, acceptance and the interior strength or confidence which results from being loved so intimately. In fact, we might even argue that such experiences are the very presupposition of Christian existence; they are experiences of salvation and we celebrate them together in every eucharist. But why then the problem, the dissatisfaction? What additional grace are we looking for?

Maybe we want a greater degree of inner peace, a surer sense of being centered. Faced with so many challenges and competing demands every day, we long for a place of quiet. Realizing that we cannot spend all of our time on retreat, we have to build a place apart within our own hearts. In that place we breathe more freely, see the details of our lives more clearly and listen to our heart's desiring more closely. None of these would be poor reasons for asking someone to teach us how to pray!

Ultimately, however, we are created for oneness with others in God. To look for God, therefore, is to look toward the world. That is why God's becoming present to us does not depend upon our discovering the right method or technique, or even the most suitable formula for prayer. There are probably many more people who have recited the Lord's prayer than have really lived it. And there are others who practiced meditation for years and applied themselves to methods of prayer, yet whose behavior was left strangely untouched by their asceticism.

To pray without ceasing, as Paul urged the Thessalonians (1 Thess 5:7), is to live from faith, not to be talking to God constantly:

> When you are praying, do not heap up empty phrases as the Gentiles do; for they think that they will be heard because of their many words. (Mt 6:7)

The whole of one's being thereby becomes a prayer, an expression of desire, gratitude, hope and compassion.

Is the World a Wilderness or a School?

As a way of describing the condition of the modern world, perhaps the image of the desert is the major one we ought to be drawing on. If the daily newspaper is any guide, the following four stories which span a mere few weeks could serve as indicators and/or reminders of how extensive and terrifying the contemporary wilderness is:

> TUZLA, Bosnia and Herzegovina, July 14—Terrorized Muslims by the tens of thousands overwhelmed aid workers in an ill-prepared emergency camp here today, part of a swelling human tide propelled by the continuing Bosnian Serb drive across eastern Bosnia.
>
> The refugees from the ostensibly protected, now conquered enclave of Srebrenica spent the day camped in open fields under a blistering sun, begging for food, water and medicine from aid workers who had little and wailing over the fates of husbands, sons, fathers and brothers taken away by Bosnian Serb forces.
>
> Their accounts of Serbian cruelty—of throats slit and women raped before the women and children were packed on buses for a mass ethnic deportation — were impossible to verify, but they held the refugees in an emotional grip.

Few of the refugees could speak of their experiences without breaking down in tears. It was all but impossible to find any who did not say they had seen evidence of atrocities or suffered them.

One distraught woman ran through the camp at mid-day, hands clutched to her head, yelling: "Stay away from me! Don't speak to me! Don't ask me anything!"

Another woman who appeared to be about 20 made her way into a grove of trees during the night and hanged herself. Her body was taken to the police station, where it remained unclaimed and unidentified.[3]

HIROSHIMA, Japan, Sunday, Aug. 6—The ones who were vaporized instantly, leaving nothing but permanent shadows on the walls behind them, they were the ones Shizuko Abe envied.

Mrs. Abe, then an 18-year-old newly-wed, was one of the unlucky survivors, broiled, irradiated and flayed, skin peeling from their bodies but not quite dead, who were witnesses when the United States ushered the world into the nuclear age 50 years ago today.

At that moment, at 8:15 on the sunny morning of Aug. 6, 1945, when the atomic bomb exploded over Hiroshima, Mrs. Abe was with some junior high school boys almost a mile from the epicenter. The blast burned her clothes off, seared her flesh and hurled her 30 feet, knocking her unconscious.

"When I came to, I looked around," she said, gently waving the claw that remains her right hand. "The boys had been so cute before, but now their clothes were burned off and they were nearly naked. Their skin was cut up and ripped off. Their faces were peeling off as well."

Though she did not know it, Mrs. Abe was herself so hideously deformed that her own parents would urge her to show mercy to her husband and leave him forever.[4]

NTARMA, Rwanda—Fifteen months ago, these 500 skulls had faces and were part of the pile of freshly killed bodies on the church floor.

A year later, with most of the flesh and hair gone, they were detached and laid in rows on the ground: round dents from hammers, thin slits from pangas, a spearpoint snapped off in an eye socket.

Two months ago, a long wooden table was built, and the skulls were rearranged on it in rows as neat as eggs. More unnerving is a second table, a tumble of blood-soaked laundry with shins and ribs sticking out.

Recently a tin roof was added, and a fence put around the site.

Slowly, carefully, and with an amateurishness that is almost touching, Rwanda is building a holocaust museum as its own Aushwitz.

All over Rwanda there are churches, schools, stadiums and public buildings like this, where Tutsi hoping for protection were trapped and massacred in April 1994. The church stories are particularly ugly. Some priests died defending their congregants. But others, including the Archbishop of Kigali, who was later killed, apparently summoned the militias when their sanctuaries were full.

The ministry has a three-phase plan: At sites of fewer than 1,000 victims—many of them in mounds of dirt thrown over the bodies by neighbors—it is having mass graves dug, lining them with plastic and reburying the dead with a proper religious ceremony. At sites of 1,000 to 10,000 victims, it does the same, but erects a sort of wooden palisade as a tomb. And in each of Rwanda's 11 prefectures, at a site of more than 10,000 victims, the Government wants some sort of shrine, so that, when the graves disappear under banana groves, no African Holocaust sceptic can say, "It never happened."[5]

EL MONTE, Calif., Aug. 3—Inside a squalid garment factory ringed with barbed wire and spiked with fences, nearly 70 foreign workers from Thailand lived and worked, sometimes for years, in what Federal agents described today as involuntary servitude.

Before the workers were freed in a pre-dawn raid by immigration officials on Wednesday, they had lived a life in which they were locked up and guarded each night and threatened with harm or death if they tried to escape. Federal officials said that the workers' children were often held hostage to insure that the parents would continue stitching together American brand-name clothes. Sometimes, the officials said, the workers were little more than children themselves.

The workers were burdened with inflated debts they could never repay, mostly for their transportation to this country, officials said. The laborers were often bused from the airport directly to the compound and, upon arrival, stripped of their possessions. They were put to work immediately, laboring long days at wages half the Federal minimum wage.[6]

The bleakness of the scenes depicted in these accounts is both more graphic and more realistic than the desert of the Sinai in which the Israelites wandered for forty years. Desert and school, needless to say, are quite different images for summing up one's experience of the world. A number of Christians from the third and fourth centuries who abandoned the world and fled to the desert of Egypt in order to find God discovered that in the end there was no escaping human nature itself. The "world" tracked them down; there were as many demons in the barren wastes of the desert as there were in the cities and towns they had left behind. Those men and women over the centuries who were not able to forsake the world physically and retreated instead to an interior enclosure were basing their religious lives on the same world-rejecting attitude. An immediate response to the four newspaper stories might be revulsion. A second, understandable reaction would be to locate and then move to a safety zone where we and our families would never come face to face with the realities behind these modern-day horror stories. We would gladly intercede for the world, but understandably might refuse ever to touch it.

Christian spirituality today is as sober as ever about the reality of sin, but its attitude toward the world is basically positive. While there might well be moments or stretches in our lives when we feel like running away from everything, we also realize that our salvation lies in engagement with the world, not in fleeing it. The children of Adam and Eve really do belong in the world, not in the security of a mythical Eden. News accounts like these are vivid reminders of the suffering countless human beings continually endure at the hands of other men and women. For those who want to find God, exiting the world is not an option.

Anyone who employs the desert image to describe today's world must bear in mind that the modern "desert" is qualitatively different from the interior wilderness which past generations of believers traversed in their thirst for life. The interior desert is always a reflection of what is taking place in the society and culture around us. The peoples of the world occupy a vastly different social and economic space than men and women did at the time of Abraham or Moses, or when the gospels were written, or during the reform movements of the sixteenth century, or even the earlier part of our own century. There is no need to spell out the moral barrenness and spiritual desolation endured by many people today; the daily newspapers will tell us that. Yet we also recall from scripture that the people of Israel came to know God in the wilderness:

> Therefore, I will now allure her,
>> and bring her into the wilderness,
>> and speak tenderly to her.
>> (Hos 2:14)

Stripped of all attachments, purified by the heat and winds that blazed across the desert sands, Israel would recover from its infidelity and again experience God.

But what precisely is the lesson of the desert? Perhaps it is that the wilderness purifies intentions and motives, breaks people's addictions to false gods, and imparts the wisdom that only one thing is truly necessary for survival, namely, "every word that comes from the mouth of God" (Mt 4:4). The desert, in other words, represents a "back to basics" experience. It also seems to teach that human nature is really fallen, that this fallenness cannot be escaped, and that fallenness is the unifying feature of human existence in every time and place. For desert Christians, woundedness becomes a true foundation of global solidarity.

The memory of the desert is also tinged with nostalgia, for the wilderness symbolized an idealized experience of first love. The desert recalls a time when all that mattered was the youthful Israel and God.

The image of the desert contains another aspect, too. Buried in the desert sands lies undreamed of potential. Thus deserts can be transformed. Isaiah writes:

> I will make a way in the wilderness,
>> and rivers in the desert.
>> (Is 43:19)

The desert thereby serves as a suggestive metaphor for

Israel's historical experience. Accordingly, God can always reverse completely the bad fortune of the people:

> For the Lord will comfort Zion;
>   he will comfort all her waste places,
> and make her wilderness like Eden,
>   her desert like the garden of the Lord;
> joy and gladness will be found in her
>   thanksgiving and the voice of song.
>
> (Is 51:3)

The wilderness into which Israel was led held the potential for a new revelation of God. Water can prod life out of the most barren wastes; God could reinvigorate people's lives, no matter how desperate their situation. If water spells life, so does justice. Again, the words of Isaiah:

> until a spirit from on high is poured out on us,
>   and the wilderness becomes a fruitful field,
>   and the fruitful field is deemed a forest.
> Then justice will dwell in the wilderness,
>   and righteousness abide in the fruitful field.
>
> (Is 32:15–16)

Without justice, there can only be despair. With justice, there is hope and the possibility of new life.

The wilderness, therefore, was a metaphor for what was taking place within the community's social, political and cultural life. The idea of the wilderness as a place of schooling goes back to Exodus. Yet while the desert could represent a time of trial, purification and learning, it could also furnish a test-case for divine power. The God of Israel could generate life even in the desert, just as God could restore people's security and well-being by raining justice upon the earth.

It is not altogether clear what prompted the "exodus"

of those Christians who renounced their worldly goods and fled to the wilderness. Some may have been fleeing the culture around them, convinced that the culture was pagan and inimical to gospel values. Some may have been looking for a challenging way to live out their faith, having been inspired by tales of the spiritual giants who had gone to the desert to wage battle with demons. Others, it has been suggested, were simply seeking to escape the burden of imperial taxes. Whatever the reasons may have been, the desert Christians of late antiquity gained a reputation for holiness. As Douglas Burton-Christie has shown, the early monastic movement was as historically complex as it was deeply spiritual, although not everyone who ran to the desert wound up both sane and saintly. Nevertheless, people could achieve enormous self-knowledge and purity of heart in the wilderness, and even today some of the sayings or teachings of the desert fathers testify to a profound insight into human nature.[7]

The image of the desert in early monasticism similarly served as a metaphor for people's historical experience. The desert became a mirror image of the world they had left behind. All the solitude on earth could not separate them from human nature itself, for with that nature went the world which had imprinted itself there. Social separation alone did not make people virtuous.

The desert of Egypt, therefore, is much more interesting as an interior space than a geographical place. It is a telling metaphor for the way many people had come to view life. One might even argue that those Christians had actually fled to the desert like pioneers in order to enter a portion of the earth rich with promise. Cultural and social life in the cities and towns of the Roman empire during late antiquity left many Christians feeling as if they were living in a spiritual wilderness. Hence the exodus. But whereas the people of Israel in their exodus from Egypt were sentenced to wander in the wilderness as punishment for faithlessness, the early monks went there both freely and eagerly. They eventually discovered, however, that the desert was more like a battleground than a sanctuary. Just as the tribes who entered the promised land found themselves waging war against the people already settled there, so too the Christians had to dispossess the demons from their desert stronghold.

I would suggest that school is a more apt metaphor than desert for describing the world, if the chief business of life is learning about God and ourselves. School encompasses most of the positive features of the desert symbol and none of the negative ones. The world itself can teach us how to relate to God and to pray, provided we take the world seriously. Many of the things which once seemed to be distractions turn out to be opportunities; many of the activities which necessarily consume our time turn out to be prayer-in-action. A person who prays but is "distracted" by concerns for family and loved ones has not thereby lost touch with God. A person who attempts to think of God but whose mind suddenly fills with scenes and sounds of suffering humanity has hardly gone off-track. And a person whose concentration upon God is abruptly shortened by the demands of the kitchen, or the neighbor in need, or the problems that daily press on men and women, shows no disrespect when attending to the intrusions.

Again, much depends upon how prayer is defined and how thoroughly faith has been integrated into the whole of one's existence. News stories like the ones above pull at our sensibilities, they provoke us into asking why such things happen, they determine the concerns we bring before God, they provoke us morally and politically, they sensitize our hearts to the dimensions of human need, they motivate us to put the gospel into practice, and they foster solidarity. The human world becomes a school for prayer. To think about union with God today apart from the experience of profound solidarity with the world would amount to a colossal misreading of the times.[8]

"Lord, Teach Us To Pray"

When the disciples made their request, they may have been looking for a formula, a new set of words to address God, which would serve as part of Jesus' spiritual legacy to them. But there is more to prayer than the language we use; indeed, many words do not make a prayer better (Mt 6:7). The words of the Lord's prayer, consequently, are intended to focus our attention on what is truly essential *and then living accordingly.* Bread is essential. Forgiving indebtedness of every kind is essential. Acknowledging the holiness and sovereignty of God is essential. The reign of God is essential.

People who prayed "Give us each day our daily bread" (Lk 11:3) never thought they did not on that account need to keep working to earn a living and support their families. They made that prayer and continued to work because they consciously depended upon God for the strength to endure. Besides, since it was God who gave the increase, bread was always regarded as a gift (2 Cor 9:10). Likewise, those who prayed "Your kingdom come" did not sit around idly, waiting for that great moment to arrive, while those who said "for we ourselves forgive everyone indebted to us" did not conclude their prayer and then simply forget what they had just promised God. Prayer was inseparable from action because praying often expressed what had to be done if indeed God's name was going to be glorified on earth or "hallowed."

Yet what the disciples' were looking for could have

taken them beyond the wording of the prayer they received
from Jesus and beyond any instruction on how to live the
spirit of that prayer. Suppose they had asked Jesus to teach
them *where* to find God. The question would hardly be
illogical for people concerned about prayer. Although the
disciples had been taught to say, "Our Father *in heaven*" (Mt
6:9), heaven would not have been the real answer to their
question.

A prophet could have answered by turning their attention toward the earth, toward this world; indeed, a prophet
might even have directed them to look toward the desert.
Not toward the desert as a geographical place from which a
lonely figure like the Baptist might have beckoned people
to conversion, but toward the many places in our world
from which people cry out to God for redemption. To ask to
be taught how to pray involves more than a search for the
right words, more than actions which will correspond to
those words, more than methods of meditation and more
than ways to examine one's conscience and renew one's
dedication, more than suitable postures or practices which
will help us center our thoughts on God. To ask the Lord to
teach us how to pray entails a willingness to seek God with
others. Matthew's version of the Lord's prayer makes this
strikingly clear: *Our* Father....Give *us* this day *our* daily
bread...forgive *us our* debts...as *we* also...*our* debtors...do
not bring *us*...but rescue *us* (Mt 6:9–13). The wording is not
"*my* Father," "*my* daily bread," "*my* debts," "bring *me*," or
"rescue *me*." Jesus expected his followers to understand
that they never stood before God alone when they prayed.

But the *we* and the *us* need to be broadened so that
they embrace *all* the others. The problem is that we might
not realize who those others are. We actually see the rest of
the worshiping community, because they are with us in
church and we live among them from day to day. Yet we

would not dare to say, "Rescue us and only us, but not all the other men and women who do not belong to our assembly, to our church, or to our nation." We would never dream of praying, "Give us our daily bread, but as for those who are not part of our community, they are your concern, not ours." The logic of the prayer, then, pulls us into an ever wider circle. God is not our Father, and only ours, but the God and Father of all.

To say to Jesus, therefore, "Teach us to pray," is to ask him to locate us in the place where we can truly know God. That place, I have suggested, is not just any place; it is specifically the place of the poor. For a Christian, it is simply impossible to divorce the world from our prayer, or to isolate our prayer from the events of history. I could never conceive of Jesus complaining to God because his prayer felt dry, but I could imagine him imploring God on behalf of those who needed bread, or release from prison, or rain for their parched fields, or the fortitude to resist corrupt judges. Such things would have been his concerns because they were the concerns of his people.

There is, in other words, an entirely distinctive sense of God one gets through solidarity with God's people, especially those people who have been heavily oppressed, betrayed, tortured and crucified. Those men and women have not been crucified with nails, but with hunger, hopelessness, terrorism, exploitation, ignorance and even self-hatred brought on by centuries of marginalization and neglect. We should not think that we could ask *Jesus* to teach us how to pray and not find ourselves pulled toward the world of the poor. Indeed, we might consult with others for guidance with our prayer, and they might encourage us to imagine God stroking us, or healing us, or leading us. They might recommend a place apart where we could engage in exercises of the spirit and develop our interior life. But if such apartness ever means distancing ourselves from the world, then we shall have walked out of the classroom.

Distractions during prayer, we have noted, can often be turned around to reveal where our hearts are really pulling us. As such, they reveal a great deal about the kind of people we are. Proceeding, as they do, from the recesses of our minds and the routines in which we live from one day to the next, distractions are certainly confirmations of our rootedness in the world, in everyday concerns, and in our bodiliness. Nothing in Christian theology that I know of would justify a body-denying attitude, for otherwise our belief in the resurrection of the body would make no sense. Why should God raise up our bodies if bodies do not count all that much? Indeed, why employ the image of a new heavens and a new earth if from the viewpoint of eternity the created world did not matter all that much?

If the everyday concerns which creep into our thoughts while we are trying to concentrate on "the things of God" are often incorrectly identified as distractions, as we have argued, then it is likewise true that sometimes the greatest distractions of all are heaven, eternity and even God! God becomes a distraction whenever we divorce God from the world which God creates, redeems and loves. Heaven becomes a distraction when detached from humanity's profound hope for the new heavens and the new earth of God's promise.

Such hope is above all the religious mark of those who hunger and thirst for justice now, whose need for bread, freedom and dignity is their constant "distraction." Christian prayer must maintain a real connectedness between the "heaven" which we trust will one day come and the existing world which stands in constant need of redemption and liberation. The insight of the fourth gospel that eternal life begins here on earth does not give us permission to reject the world and human history in favor of the heavenly glory that awaits us. Of what use is eternal life to us now, unless to enable us to embrace the world in profound and lasting solidarity? John's insight should not be allowed to justify a negative judgment about the world with which the Word of God itself has been forever joined. If new and redeemed life has already begun, then we ought always to be looking at the world with eyes of hope, convinced beyond all doubt that the human wilderness can be remade, that the forces of poverty and oppression can be defeated.

Will the World Overwhelm Us?

Life is not meant to be all pain and suffering. In fact, one way of viewing the miracles within the gospels is to think of them as signs pointing to what things will be like in the new heavens and the new earth. From the long-range perspective of Christian hope, which is rooted in the Easter conviction that the powers of darkness and death have been broken, all of creation will one day be liberated from poverty and fear and every kind of oppressive condition. In the meantime, however, Christians lead an existence which is simultaneously joyful and sober. On the one hand, no matter how terrible the situation of the world, and no matter how serious they are about living their religion, Christians are not supposed to be driven people. Our belief that the world ultimately belongs to God, and that only the Spirit creates and redeems, protects us from being overburdened and crushed by our exposure to massive human suffering. There has to be room in our lives to celebrate and be festive, even though the world's liberation is so unfinished. Meals shared with Jesus, to judge from the gospel accounts, were celebratory, joyous occasions. Those meals showed an important feature of his message about the kingdom of God, for not only were they signs of reconciliation as people sat together and shared food, but they were also acknowledgments that really good news calls for celebration.

On the other hand, countless men and women exist on the brink of survival, and many of them will simply perish. The Christian can never forget that fact, even temporarily. There is, then, a sense of great urgency that informs our lives and our prayer. The world keeps clamoring for our attention. To wonder whether the world will overwhelm us and drain our spirits is a legitimate and important concern. Within the gospels, Jesus appears as a boundary breaker. That is, Jesus is constantly challenging group assumptions about who belongs and who does not. His table fellowship with "sinners" is probably the chief illustration of the breaking of boundaries, but we notice the same thing when he touches a leper, or befriends a demon-possessed man, or identifies a Samaritan as "good."

The Jesus who keeps no boundaries when it comes to people who need a physician (Mk 2:17) may well keep pushing back or breaking the boundaries inside of us that have kept the world at a safe distance. Not only was Jesus unable to escape the crowds that tracked him down in the most out-of-the-way places; he also greeted them with compassion. The disciples may have resented the constant intrusion of the multitudes, but not Jesus. Even in our prayer we may experience the surging, challenging, humbling action of the Spirit of Jesus as defenses come down and more of the world rushes in. Will our spiritual energies be exhausted by the numbers of lives which spill into ours, by the weight of their burdens, or by the sadness of their stories? In short, will our prayer lives succumb to spiritual burnout?

The ascent to perfection or the development of the interior life has never been without its hazards and struggle. The

Christian ascetical tradition can point to numerous men and women who have pioneered various paths of the Spirit and who have bequeathed to later generations perceptive descriptions of their inner experience. Sometimes their search for God nearly ran aground in exasperation, and sometimes it seemed to turn them into religious neurotics. Common to all of them, however, was the conviction that the goal of the interior life is union with God in love. Although in some cases an individual's narrative account of his or her inner experience might not have seemed altogether orthodox, nevertheless the touchstone of authentic oneness with God was always love of neighbor, compassion and service—fruits of the Spirit.

It should not be surprising, therefore, that the prayerful search for God in our time carries certain risks. One risk, as we have said, is the possibility of being overwhelmed by the immensity of the world's suffering. Another risk would be the possibility of God and world collapsing into each other. Whenever this happens, what is left is a fascination with the world, perhaps even a "mystical" oneness with it, but a world essentially devoid of grace. For the Christian, the world with which we are in solidarity is a world daily "loved" into existence by God. God and world are by no means identical, but where prayer proceeds from solidarity the world cannot be seen without God and God cannot be seen apart from the world. What protects us against interior burnout as the heart's (and the imagination's) boundaries get pushed to the limit is our experience that God is with the world, always. But this lesson can only be learned through constant engagement with the world, not by retreating from its demands.

11

The Future of Spirituality and the Option for the Poor

In matters of the Spirit, it is undeniably true that the quest for the transcendent and a richer interior life has assumed many forms over the centuries. To speak only of our particular tradition, Christianity itself emerged amidst a swirl of charismatic movements and beliefs, most of which disappeared during the process in which the "great tradition" (as it has sometimes been called) took shape. Periodically throughout the history of the church, renewal movements have arisen, often with the purpose of renewing and reforming church belief and practice. Sometimes these very movements became formally structured and entered the mainstream of Christian life as religious orders or religious communities. Not infrequently, however, sincere efforts to reform the church ran aground in spent enthusiasm, mistaken notions about the gospel, emotion and pride, or even ecclesiastical suspicion and hard-headedness.

Movements are not always easy to authenticate. In the case of my own religious community, for example, Ignatius Loyola's insistence that Jesuits would not recite the divine office in common the way monks had traditionally prayed it in choir caused many churchmen to question Ignatius' vision of religious life. And there was, it seemed, a perennial difficulty in understanding how Ignatius' spiritual insight, embedded in his *Spiritual Exercises*, was different from the claims of the alumbrados or illuminists, who were frequent targets of the Spanish inquisition. Ignatius himself was arrested at several points in his career. He was not the only founder of a religious group to run into problems with church authorities.[1]

It is fair to say that in the case of religious movements and new insights into life according to the Spirit there needs always to be a church-wide discernment. But here it would be a mistake to make correctness of belief the *primary* criterion of whether or not the Spirit of God is at work. A person who would have vigorously advocated frequent confession in the early church, for instance, would have been acting outside the apostolic tradition and condemned as an innovator. Today, on the other hand, anyone who might argue that a true Christian should never have to make use of sacramental confession, because a fully committed Christian would never fall into grave sin, is likely to be censured.[2] The *primary* criterion of whether or not something is of God has to be fixed in terms of everyday practice. Most of us would agree that wherever we find love, compassion, efforts at building communion through reconciliation and peace-making, or forgiveness, there we detect the finger of God driving demons out of our world (Lk 11:20). There we recognize the Spirit at work.

What about the option for the poor, the idea which has been hovering behind every page thus far? That the option for the poor is of the Spirit we should have no doubt; there is certainly no question about its orthodoxy. But is it fair to say that Christian spirituality for the foreseeable future will be inseparably connected with our making a preferential option for the poor both as individuals and as believing communities? We are not just talking about a theological innovation, a devotional practice, a method of prayer or a pastoral strategy. The option for the poor concerns who and what we are as people baptized into Christ Jesus. The need to rethink every dimension of Christian spirituality—our liturgical life, our forms of piety, our ascetical practices, our way of relating to one another and to God, our way of reading scripture, our prayer—is not going to pass away until there is no more poverty, no more injustice and violence, and no more despair on the face of the earth. The option for the poor is another way of phrasing the petition from the Lord's prayer, "Your kingdom come."

In contemporary religious writing we find a growing number of what I would call "regional spiritualities": creation spirituality with its attention upon the environment, feminist spiritualities with its justice-driven concern for gender issues and its theological insight, born of women's experience, into the nature of God, liberationist spiritualities developed from within the worlds of black and Latino experience, spiritualities developed for people suffering from AIDS, or for the elderly, ecumenical spirituality for people engaged in inter-religious dialogue, and so forth. Each has something to offer to the wider church, to enrich our common religious heritage. The option for the poor, however, is actually none of these, for it is not a regional spirituality. It comes from the heart of the gospel itself, and therefore we should call it evangelical. In fact, the option for the poor has to cut across every regional spirituality in order to prevent it from spinning off into its own solitary orbit.

In addition, the option for the poor generates its own form of asceticism or "spiritual discipline."[3] For those of us living in a consumer-oriented society, a real discipline will be required if our souls are not to be swept along in a mad rush to buy, to possess, to throw away. But asceticism is not simply a matter of adopting counter-cultural values or bucking the tide of a consumerist society, at least not from a gospel standpoint. It involves more than energetic efforts at recycling and changing one's diet to include more vegetables and less red meat. The spirituality generated by the option for the poor even goes beyond a "compassionate sensibility" for the pain of others.[4] It will certainly require a degree of alertness to events in our world and a readiness to change one's lifestyle. Should we buy clothing from a company that grossly underpays its workers, say, in El Salvador, or coffee from companies which might exploit the labor of, say, poor Indians in Guatemala, or lettuce and grapes from producers who take advantage, say, of migrant farm workers in California? A passionate concern for justice would be an appropriate contemporary expression of Christian asceticism. Christian spirituality today has to be prophetic.[5]

But the asceticism which comes from the option for the poor ultimately has to move us radically in their direction. The key word here might be solidarity, but solidarity in the concrete, and not merely in the abstract. "Vital contact with the reality of injustice," said the U.S. bishops. Inserting oneself into the world of the poor is by no means easy, and it will not leave us feeling comfortable. Imagine how we would feel if we passed our parents waiting for a meal from a soup kitchen, or if we saw one of our children begging from people on the street! Our parents and our children belong to us. What then will happen when we begin to view the world's poor as truly our sisters and brothers, every bit as much related to us as our blood relatives? What sort of challenges will this create? What sort of resistances? What will be the nature of our distractions then while we pray? How would we feel sitting down to eat, knowing our parents were standing in line at a shelter? Would we have the same reaction, knowing that so many other men and women are suffering? What works of justice will our moral sensibilities lead us to undertake? What sort of politicians will it make of us, or executives, or bankers, or teachers? What kind of research will it bring us to undertake? What sort of human being will the option for the poor make of us? It will make us, as Paul says, like the one who emptied himself and took the form of a servant.

Finally, the option for the poor is not presented to us as a fresh moral burden or yet another occasion for feeling sinful and guilty about the kind of people that we are. If that were the case, the gospel itself would not be good news; it would be a message calculated to make our souls perpetually miserable. The option for the poor always presupposes that men and women are sincerely looking for God, and thus one does not make such an option apart from a desire to learn how to pray with and in the Spirit of Jesus.

I ought to add, however, that while the option for the poor does not lead us to invent a brand new category of sin, it could well bring us to experiencing within ourselves the sin of the world. By this stage of our lives, most of us know only too well our individual spiritual and moral limitations; personal sinfulness is hardly something foreign to the religious sensibility of an adult Christian.

Yet solidarity with the world by its very nature includes a sense of connectedness with the sinfulness of the world, a sinfulness which is in part mine and in large part not mine, yet which I shall always carry within me. Those who did not know this kind of sin before making the option for the poor will certainly know it afterward. Here we may not be too far from Paul's idea that God made Christ who did not know sin to be sin, "so that in him we might become the righteousness of God" (2 Cor 5:21). If the twin scourge of poverty and violence, and every other form of human wretchedness, were things I did not know before encountering the world of the poor, I know them now. What is more, I shall never be able to live again as if I had not met that world.

The great mystery of reconciliation begins deep inside of us, certainly through our accepting the offer of divine mercy God extends to each of us personally, but above all through our willingness, indeed our desire, to be reconciled with the world. Fundamental spiritual estrangement takes two forms: the estrangement of the individual human being from God, and, just as importantly, the estrangement of an individual man or woman from the world of the poor. The person who has made the option for the poor will never run out of meaningful sins to confess and to place before God, because the sinfulness which he or she feels and expresses is at the same time the sin of the world. *That* sin and *that* moral woundedness will need forgiveness and healing until the end of the ages. Furthermore, the one who lives in solidarity with the world realizes profoundly that his or her own reconciliation and redemption will remain radically incomplete until the whole world is finally reconciled to God.

What Option Do the Poor Make?

Now, if the church views itself as called to make a preferential option for the poor, to what are the poor themselves called? Is nothing demanded of them? The issue is an important one. If the future of Christian spirituality is closely tied to the whole church's making an option for the poor, and if the poor make up the vast majority of the world's population, are we speaking merely about a spirituality for those privileged Christians who have made it politically, socially and economically?

To answer this question we need first to remind ourselves that there is nothing spiritually romantic about the moral or religious state of the poor *qua* poor. Poverty hurts. It is frequently dehumanizing and always destructive of the human potential for happiness and life. Just consider its effects on children and their families, villages and communities, even whole regions and countries. But if the gospel message were identical for everyone, then the call to repentance would fall disproportionately hard on men and women whose capacity for hearing the gospel is already impaired by the desperate circumstances in which they are forced to live. Stealing may be against the law, but I can readily understand why someone whose family needs food or clothing or medicine would be forced to take what he or she needs. In fact, I can think of any number of conditions which might lead to a breakdown in the human values we respect and cherish. But to expect those who live below any reasonable standard of living, who barely survive from one day to the next and whose life expectancy is much shorter than ours, to be models of civic virtue would be unfair. To be sure, the gospel calls all of us to repentance, rich and poor alike. But does repentance spell the same thing in both cases?

The book of Job may be instructive here. The premise of Satan's strategy in the introductory scenes of the book is that people suffering desperately are more likely to curse God, while those richly blessed may be nothing more than fair-weather friends. It was assumed that those afflicted with terrible misfortune, such as the poor and the oppressed, would be less likely to follow the moral imperatives of God's law. Job was righteous, Satan had argued, because he was rich and lived among the privileged class. Yet this argument gives us away, does it not? The afflicted of the earth can plead a defense which the well-off cannot deploy. The problem with the poor is not that they are wretched sinners and more likely to fall into sin than those who can afford to live righteously. Rather, their problem is that their capacity for hope gets paralyzed by poverty and all its attendant demons.

Maybe where the gospel today calls for an option for the poor on the part of those who are well off, it calls for something entirely different from the poor themselves. After all, no one opts for poverty. In the case of the poor, their option has to become an option for hope, for how could we imagine Jesus' preaching the kingdom of God as good news to the poor unless he was awakening people's hope? I think I could preach and teach, without stumbling or hesitating, that the gospel asks the poor to make an option for the kingdom. But I could only do so credibly and sincerely on the basis of a real solidarity with the poor on my part. And so too the whole church. The church can call the poor to make an option for the kingdom of God, which is an option for hope, only if together we have made a decision to stand with the poor, and only if that decision is evidenced in the way that we act. More often than not, however, the poor themselves may be the ones who will give us insight into what the kingdom of God means, as the following story shows:

> HATTIESBURG, Miss. Aug. 10—Oseola McCarty spent a lifetime making other people look nice. Day after day, for most of her 87 years, she took in bundles of dirty clothes and made them clean and neat for parties she never attended, weddings to which she was never invited, graduations she never saw.
>
> She had quit school in the sixth grade to go to work, never married, never had children and never learned to drive because there was never any place in particular she wanted to go. All she ever had was the work,

which she saw as a blessing. Too many other black people in rural Mississippi did not have even that.

She spent almost nothing, living in her old family home, cutting the toes out of shoes if they did not fit right and binding her ragged Bible with Scotch tape to keep Corinthians from falling out. Over the decades, her pay—mostly dollar bills and change—grew to more than $150,000.

"More than I could ever use," Miss McCarty said the other day without a trace of self-pity. So she is giving her money away, to finance scholarships for black students at the University of Southern Mississippi here in her hometown, where tuition is $2,400 a year.

"I wanted to share my wealth with the children," said Miss McCarty, whose only real regret is that she never went back to school. "I never minded work, but I was always so busy, busy. Maybe I can make it so the children don't have to work like I did."[6]

Two Necessary Virtues

Letting the world teach us how to pray requires two special virtues. We need patience, and we need hope.

Patience is not an easy virtue for people who have grown accustomed to reliability, efficiency and quick solutions. The accomplishments of modern technology and engineering, affecting every area of our lives, deceive us into thinking that the world is supposed to run smoothly and efficiently, and according to our calendars and clocks. What used to take hours and weeks of labor can now be concluded within moments, thanks to computers. Trips that might have required months of travel can now be made within hours. We are, of course, pretty adaptable; and when waiting becomes inevitable, we may fume but eventually we adjust our interior clocks. Sometimes we are even surprised by the lesson to be learned from an enforced delay, breakdown or cancellation. The recovery of independence is often a grace, although none of us would probably want to renounce the physical advantages of modern life.

But is that what patience is all about? Just as wisdom is more than common sense, patience is more than being able to wait when we have no choice. Patience is not unrelated to suffering: not just an enforced waiting, which one accepts with resignation, but a waiting with longing. Or even better, patience is a waiting in hope. Given the enormity of the world's problems, one has to abandon any expectation of resolving all the issues quickly. Yet neither can we merely grit our teeth and try to find something to distract us momentarily, like people caught in a traffic snarl. A person of patience is not one who resigns himself to the inevitable, because patience is not a passive virtue. Patience is the way we suffer through something even while we are fully engaged. We do not give up: even if physically we are incapable of doing very much, our minds and hearts—our praying—remain active and alive, longing and trusting.

For this reason, patience and hope are joined to one another. Apart from hope, patience could degenerate into resignation, and resignation into despair. But to stay committed and to continue working, despite the fact that what we seek is going to remain unrealized for a long time, requires more than determination and rugged wills. Hope, then, is the great virtue for those who take history to heart, those who continually feel and cherish our common humanity. Hope is not believing in a fiction, like someone who sets an imaginary goal so as not to surrender to disenchantment and death. For Christians, at any rate, hope is rooted in the faith that despite everything the world still belongs to God. The resurrection, we have seen, remakes the human wilderness. Hope, we are now saying, is what defines patience as Christian. Perhaps it is this note of patience suffused with hope which the author of the second letter of Peter had in mind when he wrote:

> Since all these things are to be dissolved in this way, what sort of persons ought you to be in leading lives of holiness and godliness, waiting for and hastening the coming of the day of God....But, in accordance with his promise, we wait for new heavens and a new earth, where righteousness is at home. (2 Pet 3:11–13)

Afterword: Inching Toward the Year 2000

Writing a book is something like organizing a yard sale. What one person considers a treasure may look to another like a candidate for the dumpster. Some people are downright addicted to rummaging through yard sales and flea markets, maybe like the merchant of the gospel story always on the lookout for that pearl of great price (Mt 13:45–46). I should be most indebted to yard sale addicts if I were organizing one, even as I am most grateful to readers with the patience to pick through pages of a book on prayer, convinced that there must be something of value within.

I remember reading about the couple who eyed an elegantly framed but nondescript painting in front of an old farm house. They bought it for the frame. But when they went to remove the parchment backing, they discovered, if memory serves me correctly, nothing less than one of the original copies of the Declaration of Independence! A stray idea in a book can be like that. Something an author takes for granted becomes suddenly and mysteriously priceless in a reader's eyes, while an idea over which one has labored for months goes begging for attention. Like an item which he figured would fetch a handsome price, at the end of the day it is still sitting on the table.

There is no such thing as the universal book. No writer can address the needs and interests of every conceivable audience. The point is so obvious that a reader could miss some of its direct applications. We might fault a writer for not sticking to his express intention or aims in setting ideas to paper, or for not writing clearly, or for being in error. But we ought not fault him for failing to address every possible angle on a given topic; for there can be as many angles to an issue as there are readers.

Someone might ask, for example, how a person could possibly write a book about prayer without ever discussing the eucharist, while another might wonder how one could write about the interior life without taking into account the Trinity. And many might ask how a person could write on any aspect of spirituality today without taking into account issues of feminism, inter-religious dialogue, sexuality, social justice, the environment, and so forth.

Yet to look at the matter a bit differently, the fact that a Christian writes about Islam or Buddhism does not mean that he or she is less committed to Christian belief and practice than, say, a New Testament scholar, even if the author never mentions Jesus in his or her writing. The fact that the gospel has practically nothing to say about the environment does not mean that Christian spirituality is ecologically blind. The author of the letter of James gives us a marvelous message about the moral life with only two incidental mentions of Christ, and that author made it into the New Testament!

Thus the point is probably worth repeating. No one can compose a universal text, not even the Holy Spirit! The bible probably comes closest to any major religious work to being "universal." It is available in nearly every language spoken around the globe. Still, even in the case of the bible there are parts which speak to us and some parts which do not. Even as a major religious text, the bible does not say everything that we might want or need to hear about God, prayer, the interior life, or even about morality. For instance, looking in the pages of the bible for solutions to complex medical-moral issues or to balancing the federal budget would be futile. The bible does not answer every question people might come up with about Jesus, revelation, our relationship with other world religions, the church, or the Trinity. And not even those great prayers of Israel known as the psalms capture every dimension of humanity's religious experience and spiritual quest.

But just as there cannot be a universal text, neither is there a universal reader. Writers naturally prefer to reach the widest audience they can. Audiences, however, are by nature limited. Not everyone wonders about the same issues; not everyone is concerned about the same set of problems, at least not concerned enough to try to do something about them. When it comes to religious matters, it goes without saying that there is a broad spectrum of appetites and tastes. The point came home to me one afternoon when a local bookstore graciously invited me to be on hand to autograph a book I had just published. As I stood next to a pile of copies, a number of customers approached, fingered the display copy, smiled politely, and then reached toward a nearby shelf for some titles on angels and Marian apparitions.

The universal reader does not exist. This means not only that a writer cannot take absolutely every particular background and living situation into consideration. It also means that there is no universal set of concerns and there is no universally relevant body of religious truths to match those concerns. In brief, a writer cannot write for everybody, because not everybody wants or needs to hear the same thing. And while I believe that an important insight or truth can be expressed in a variety of ways, to meet the particularities of a variety of individuals and groups, I am not sure that the universality of such truths and insights is as evident as religious people often claim.

Several years ago, the religious writer Paul Knitter suggested that the language which Christians use of Jesus might be compared to love-language. When a husband claims that his wife is the most beautiful woman in the world, he has no way empirically of verifying his claim, nor would anyone expect him to try. We accept what he says because we understand the sort of language he is using. Similarly, when Christians maintain that Jesus is the absolute savior and that only through his name will all men and women find salvation, as we hear in Acts 4:12—

> There is salvation in no one else, for there is no other
> name under heaven given among mortals by which
> we must be saved

—they are closer to love-language than scientific language.[1] Not everyone would necessarily agree that he or she needs a savior, and it would be impossible to verify whether some human beings, perhaps many, had been "lost" because they never shared faith in Christ. The church today, of course, is hardly fundamentalist with respect to New Testament claims. It has learned to nuance its positions with respect to other faiths, the necessity of baptism for salvation, and so on. Yet the fact remains that what might purport to be universally valid religious truth frequently turns out, in the end, to reveal more about us than about God.

All of this is said by way of caution and explanation. It is not possible, when talking about prayer and the interior life, to meet everyone's expectations. What I can hope is that the ideas I have developed here will make sense to at least a few other Christians who have found themselves wondering about the state of belief as we come to the close of the second millennium.

What Is Special About the Year 2000?

There is nothing magical about numbers, of course. Whatever fascination there is about the number 2000 has to be largely symbolic and western. If I have calculated correctly, for Hindus the year 2000 according to the Common Era (and the Gregorian calendar), which dates time from the birth of Christ, will be the year 2057 of Vikrim Samvat. For some Buddhist societies it will be the year 2543, marking time since the Buddha's birth, while our year 2000 will be the year 1421 on the Islamic calendar, which dates from the prophet Muhammad's Hegira or emigration from Mecca to Medina in 622 C.E. For the Bahai faith, the year 2000 will be 157 B.E. (Bahai Era). What makes the turn of the millennium significant is the sum of cultural, social, economic, political, technological, historical and religious forces which have brought us to what has been widely (and, I think, infelicitously) referred to as the "post-modern era." The human race, in other words, is stepping into a very different social and cultural space. The year number on its calendars is quite irrelevant.

But let us be honest. There is something disturbing in the air which makes us nervous and afraid of entering into that new space. For one thing, the intellectual security that religious convictions used to afford us seems to be foundering on the shoals of history. The scriptures, we realize, did not fall from the heavens. They were composed by human authors, and these authors were both creative and limited. The more we have learned about the circumstances surrounding the composition of the biblical writings, the more we have had to rethink what divine revelation is all about. As I have tried to explain, there is no point in looking outside of history for a revelation which will stabilize our sense of the divine. God comes to us from within the human story, not outside of it.

What is probably a lot more unsettling, however, is our sense that the world is sinking, or at least being swamped, as a result of so many large and seemingly intractable problems. It is not just that we watch, read or hear about tragedy and suffering; natural disasters, accidents and violence have always been a part of human history. What is so frightening is the awful scale of human misfortune, the swelling population of the earth's poor, the unbearable strain being put on the planet's finite resources, the blindness and greed of a powerful minority, and the growing number of people who do not seem to care. It has been estimated that by the year 2050 there may be ten to eleven billion people inhabiting the earth, perhaps more. According to one analysis:

> Of the many implications of this global trend, four stand out—at least with respect to our inquiry. The first and most important is that 95 percent of the twofold increase in the world's population expected before the middle of the next century will occur in poor countries, especially those least equipped to take the strain. Second, although globally the relative share of human beings in poverty is expected to shrink, in absolute numbers there will be far more poor people on earth in the early twenty-first century than ever before, unless serious intervention occurs. Third, within the Third World a greater and greater percentage of the population is drifting from the countryside into gigantic shanty-cities. Even by the

end of this decade São Paulo is expected to contain 22.6 million people, Bombay 18.1 million, Shanghai 17.4 million, Mexico City 16.2 million, and Calcutta 12.7 million—all cities that run the risk of becoming centers of mass poverty and social collapse....And fourth, these societies are increasingly adolescent in composition—in Kenya in 1985, to take an extreme case, 52 percent of the population was under fifteen— and the chances that their resource-poor governments will be able to provide education and jobs for hundreds of millions of teenagers are remote.[2]

The political, economic and social circumstances of our time place a terrible burden on those who are trying to hold on to their belief that the God who created the world is good and has not abandoned us to our own devices. For those of us who live in the First World, few things can be as devastating as the sudden loss of work. Corporate mergers and downsizing have caused a great deal of social and financial dislocation among those who had grown accustomed to a secure, predictable and comfortable way of life. Many people who had invested a great deal of energy and trust in corporate giants have found themselves sadly disillusioned, and without jobs. What vast numbers of men and women have been experiencing constantly, namely, the unfairness which is very much a part of free-market economies, has begun to strike home. No longer can parents be confident that their children will have economically brighter futures than they did.

Being a person of faith as the church approaches the year 2000 is not going to get easier; indeed, it will probably get harder. This book represents one person's effort to think about how Christian spirituality is being affected by the times.[3] It cannot say everything which ought to be said, and some readers may well conclude that I have started with a miserably incomplete grasp of the situation in which we find ourselves today. Nevertheless, we have no choice but to keep thinking and wrestling, praying and speaking with one another, studying and writing, even when what we come up with is more probative and searching than firm and final.

We used to hear it said occasionally that there was no such thing as "cheap grace." By that we meant something like "no pain, no gain," if we were serious about developing as people of faith. Life continually challenges us; it stretches our patience, our courage, our capacity for forgiveness and love, our readiness to hope, and our ability to be rigorously honest with ourselves. There is no easy route to individual holiness, and there are countless strategies for evading Christian adulthood. Just as Jesus learned obedience through suffering, so also each and every believer makes his or her way to God gradually and through the purifying, humbling process of growing up, provided we earnestly want to become fully free and responsible men and women.

But we need to expand the idea. The challenges we face are not only the private, individual everyday setbacks, problems, weariness, anxieties, and so forth that each of us knows only too well. There are also the society-wide tensions, ambiguities, fears and uncertainties which in one way or another intrude into our private, everyday worlds. One might not like to think about genocide and starvation in Africa, or the manufacture and deployment of land-mines, or welfare reform, or the plight of migrant farm workers from Mexico, or massacres in Guatemala, or refugees in Bosnia. But issues like these impinge upon all of us economically, politically, morally and spiritually.

The gospel tells us that Jesus on the mountainside had directed his followers to pray, "And do not bring us to the time of trial" (Mt 5:13). Likewise in the garden he would instruct his disciples to pray, "Keep awake and pray that you may not come into the time of trial" (Mk 14:38). Perhaps the assault or "trial" we shall have to endure at the beginning of the next century is going to be against our readiness to hope. In order to survive that trial we shall need every resource our faith can make available to us. I believe that even now our faith, the faith of the people of God, is being tried and tested:

> …so that the genuineness of your faith—being more precious than gold that, though perishable, is tested by fire—may be found to result in praise and glory and honor when Jesus Christ is revealed. (1 Pet 1:7)

And yet even now, while we have been conversing with one another in these pages, the Spirit is planting seeds for the future, readying hearts and imaginations to face formidable odds with a hope firmly, deeply rooted in the story of Jesus.

In a beautiful, moving essay, Alice Walker recounts the moment when her young daughter first noticed the deformity in one of her mother's eyes. Expecting that the little girl, lying in her crib and staring at her mother's face, would react in horror, the mother braced herself for rejection. What came was a cry of delight: "Mommy, there's a *world* in your eye.…Mommy, where did you *get* that world in your eye?" At that moment she discovered, Walker confides to us, that it was even possible to love the damaged eye which had caused her so much shame and anger ever since she was a child.[4]

The words of that little girl might serve as a description of what it is going to mean to be Christian in the year 2000. Christians will be people who have the world in their eye. The very reality which we would flee or deny can suddenly become a blessing. For the truth is that each of us carries some measure of the world's woundedness inside of us, and each of us must reckon with that reality and allow God to heal us. It can be a moment of great grace to feel one's connectedness with the world at the very point we least suspected, the point where we know ourselves most damaged: the point of our weakness, our powerlessness, our yearning for deliverance, our desire to belong to the whole human race. *Mommy, there's a world in your eye.* These words seem to capture a profound spiritual insight. The Christian never stands apart from the world, but always within it. What greater compliment could anyone pay us than to tell us that the world can be seen in our eyes? After all, the eye reflects what the heart desires.

Notes

Introduction

1. See H. Saddhatissa, *The Life of the Buddha* (San Francisco: Harper & Row, 1976).

2. The story of Moses can be found in Exodus 2.

3. See Michel Carrouges, *Soldier of the Spirit: The Life of Charles de Foucauld* (New York: G. P. Putnam's Sons, 1956), 116.

4. See Eileen Egan, *Such a Vision of the Street: Mother Teresa—The Spirit and the Work* (Garden City, NY: Doubleday & Co., 1985), 16–44.

5. See Thomas Merton, *Conjectures of a Guilty Bystander* (Garden City, NY: Doubleday & Co., 1966), 140–141.

6. Jean-Yves Calvez, *Faith and Justice: The Social Dimension of Evangelization* (St. Louis: The Institute of Jesuit Sources, 1991), 97.

7. The texts are quoted from Norman P. Tanner, ed., *Decrees of the Ecumenical Councils* (Washington, DC: Georgetown University Press, 1990), volume 2. Emphasis added.

8. See *The Gospel of Peace and Justice: Catholic Social Teaching since Pope John*, presented by Joseph Gremillion (Maryknoll, NY: Orbis Books, 1976), 514.

9. Ibid., 524.

10. See James Empereur and Christopher Kiesling, *The Liturgy That Does Justice* (Collegeville: The Liturgical Press, 1990).

11. U.S. Bishops, *Economic Justice for All: Pastoral Letter on Catholic Social Teaching and the U.S. Economy* (Washington, DC: United States Catholic Conference, 1986), 45.

12. See Donal Dorr, "Solidarity and Integral Human Development" in *The Logic of Solidarity: Commentaries on John Paul II's Encyclical "On Social Concern,"* ed. Gregory Baum and Robert Ellsberg (Maryknoll: Orbis Books, 1989), 143–154. Also, Jon Sobrino, "Bearing with One Another in Faith: A Theological Analysis of Christian Solidarity," in *The Principle of Mercy: Taking the Crucified People from the Cross* (Orbis Books, 1994), 144–172.

13. This point has also been made by Luke Timothy Johnson in *The Real Jesus: The Misguided Quest for the Historical Jesus and the Truth of the Traditional Gospels* (San Francisco: HarperSanFrancisco, 1996).

14 Gerard Manley Hopkins, "The Wreck of the Deutschland," fifth stanza, in *The Poems of Gerard Manley Hopkins*, ed. W. H. Gardner and N. H. MacKenzie (London: Oxford University Press, 1967), 53.

15. For this passage from her final letter I am indebted to a contribution by Friedrich Wulf in Herbert Vorgrimler, ed., *Commentary on the Documents of Vatican II* (New York: Herder & Herder, 1968), vol. 2:330.

16. Sebastian Moore, *The Crucified Jesus Is No Stranger* (New York: Seabury Press, 1977; reprinted by Paulist Press), and C. S. Song, *Jesus, The Crucified People* (New York: Crossroad Publishing Co., 1990; reprinted by Augsburg Fortress).

1. Letting the World Pray Through Us

1. Several popular collections are *The Oxford Book of Prayer*, ed. George Appleton (Oxford: Oxford University Press, 1985); *Conversations with God: Two Centuries of Prayers by African Americans*, ed. James Melvin Washington (New York: HarperCollins, 1994); *The HarperCollins Book of Prayers*, compiled by Robert Van de Weyer (New York: HarperCollins, 1993).

2. See St. Thomas Aquinas, *Summa Theologiae*, edited and translated by Kevin D. O'Rourke (New York: McGraw-Hill Book Company, 1964), 39:49, 51. Aquinas' treatment of prayer occurs in Question 83 of the *Summa*. The text Aquinas is citing can be found in Book Three of Saint John of Damascus' work *Orthodox Faith*, where John's concern is actually Jesus' prayer. "He became a model for us, He taught us to ask of God and to lift ourselves up to Him, and through His sacred mind He opened the way for us to ascend to God." See Saint John of Damascus, *Writings*, trans. Frederick H. Chase, Jr., volume 37 in the series *The Fathers of the Church* (New York: Fathers of the Church, Inc., 1958), 329.

3. *St. Thérèse of Lisieux: An Autobiography* (New York: P. J. Kenedy & Sons, 1926), 180. See the *Catechism of the Catholic Church* (Mahwah: Paulist Press, 1994), 613.

4. *Catechism*, 613–615.

5. "Neither prayer nor any other virtuous deed is meritorious without sanctifying grace. However, even that prayer which impetrates sanctifying grace proceeds from some grace as from a gratuitous gift, because the very act of praying is *a gift of God*, as Augustine states." *Summa*, 39:93.

6. For example, see Patrick D. Miller, *They Cried to the Lord: The Form and Theology of Biblical Prayer* (Minneapolis: Fortress Press, 1994).

7. James Melvin Washington, *Conversations with God: Two Centuries of Prayers by African Americans* (New York: HarperCollins, 1994), xxx–xxxi.

8. See the entry under "Prayer" in *The New Dictionary of Catholic Spirituality*, ed. Michael Downey (Collegeville, MN: The Liturgical Press, 1993). The text cited appears on p. 775.

9. See Karl Rahner, *Prayers for a Lifetime*, ed. Albert Raffelt and newly reprinted (New York: The Crossroad Publishing Co., 1995). The theological tone aside, Rahner's "style" here is not that much different from what we would find in traditional prayer books and devotionals.

10. Pedro Casaldáliga and José-María Vigil, *Political Holiness: A Spirituality of Liberation* (Maryknoll, NY: Orbis Books, 1994), 178. For a set of matching prayers to this book see the little collection of Luis Espinal, *Oraciones a quemarropa* (Sucre, Bolivia: Qori Llama, 1981). Unfortunately, it is not available in English.

11. Karl Rahner wrote: "Love of God and love of neighbor stand in a relationship of mutual conditioning. Love of neighbor is not only a love that is demanded by the love of God, an achievement flowing from it; it is also in a certain sense its antecedent condition." (*The Practice of Faith: A Handbook of Contemporary Spirituality* [New York: The Crossroad Publishing Co., 1983], 136.) But Rahner left the category of neighbor less defined than I have. The neighbor is not an abstraction, any more than God is. However, the neighbor is not just anyone. Above all, the neighbor is the one who is in need, indeed all those who fall into the hands of the robbers of this world, like the poor man of the gospel story. See also his book *The Love of Jesus and the Love of Neighbor* (New York: Crossroad, 1983).

12. One finds this regularly in his commentary on the Psalms. See Saint Augustine, *Exposition on the Book of*

Psalms in *A Select Library of the Nicene and Post-Nicene Fathers*, ed. Philip Schaff, Volume VIII (New York: The Christian Literature Company, 1888).

13. Karen Armstrong, *A History of God: The 4000-Year Quest of Judaism, Christianity and Islam* (New York: Alfred A. Knopf, 1993).

14. Jack Miles, *God: A Biography* (New York: Alfred A. Knopf, 1995). The book was awarded a Pulitzer prize.

15. For a Christian, perhaps more jarring than seeing God as a literary character or historical actor is to discover Jesus reduced to his sayings. See John Dominic Crossan, *The Essential Jesus: Original Sayings and Earliest Images* (San Francisco: HarperSanFrancisco, 1994). Without the stories to hold and situate them, the sayings are lifeless, anchored in no one's experience, the timeless aphorisms of a wise man. That may be one reason why the early communities preferred to hand Jesus' sayings along in the form of the gospels.

16. For many people the word "mystic" is basically positive. In a splendid essay entitled "The Spirituality of the Church of the Future," the Jesuit theologian Karl Rahner wrote that "the Christian of the future will be a mystic or he will not exist at all." Nevertheless, "mystic" also suggests apartness (Rahner speaks of "the solitary Christian"). Where Rahner speaks of the mystic, I would substitute the term "contemplative." See Karl Rahner, *Concern for the Church* [*Theological Investigations*, volume 20] (New York: The Crossroad Publishing Co., 1981), 149.

17. Evelyn Underhill's book *Mysticism: The Preeminent Study in the Nature and Development of Spiritual Consciousness* (originally published in 1911 and reprinted by Doubleday [New York, 1990]) remains a standard text. It seems to me, however, that were one to be writing that book today, one might begin with the supposition that the

"development of spiritual consciousness" cannot be a private, solitary affair if we are talking about a properly Christian growth in the Spirit. This insight would recast the way we think about purification, asceticism, forms of prayer, and so forth. Similarly, we might fine-tune Karl Rahner's comments about everyday mysticism, especially in light of his belief that the Christian of the future would have to be a mystic.

18. Armstrong, 397–398, 399.

19. Miles, 397–408.

2. Faith Without Solidarity Is Dead

1. I do not want to get into the question of the possible historical connection between Paul and James. Nevertheless, since both authors appear in the New Testament, it is reasonable to expect a reader to view one in thematic relationship to the other. See Luke Timothy Johnson, *The Letter of James* (New York: Doubleday, 1995), 246.

2. James Hamilton-Paterson, *Ghosts of Manila* (New York: Farrar, Straus & Giroux, 1994), 123.

3. The council declared: "Nor does divine Providence deny the help necessary for salvation to those who, without blame on their part, have not yet arrived at an explicit knowledge of God, but who strive to live a good life, thanks to His grace." From the *Dogmatic Constitution on the Church*, #16 (*The Documents of Vatican II*, ed. Walter Abbott [New York: The America Press, 1966], 35).

4. Susan Griffin, *A Chorus of Stones: The Private Life of War* (New York: Doubleday, 1992), 9, 38.

5. V. S. Naipaul, *A Way in the World* (New York: Alfred A. Knopf, 1994), 11.

3. The Election of Israel or the Adoption of the Poor?

1. For an excellent recent study of early efforts to make sense of Jesus' death, see John T. Carroll and Joel B. Green, *The Death of Jesus in Early Christianity* (Peabody, MA: Hendrickson Publishers, 1995).

2. "Yet, of course, the thought [adoption] is clearly present in the Hebrew scriptures...evoking the folk memory of that initial great act of redemption whereby God took the children of Israel as his own (Ex 4:22; Hos 11:1)." See James D. G. Dunn, *Romans 9–16* (Dallas: Word Books, 1988 [*Word Biblical Commentary*, volume 38b]), 533.

3. Again to quote Dunn: "To break the link between the old and new covenant is not to liberate his [Paul's] gospel but to destroy it, for his gospel is nothing if it is not the continuation and fulfillment of all that God intended for and through his chosen people" (535).

4. I say this because some may not want to accept the implication. *True* is not a property of religion as such, as if the propositions of a particular religion were *true* because *revealed*. *True* is better viewed as a property of the human response to God's offer of grace and salvation. Thus, all religions are derivatively "true" if they mediate God's offer of grace. I think we should be cautious about using the word "true" to refer to our religion or to the church, lest we thereby suggest that other faiths or churches are false. I comment on the term "revelation" in the next chapter. For a helpful discussion, see Schubert M. Ogden, *Is There Only One True Religion or Are There Many?* (Dallas: Southern Methodist University Press, 1992), 99ff.

5. The way we think about salvation is vital to the way we read and appropriate the gospel story. For a recent study, see Dean Brackley, *Divine Revolution: Salvation &*

Liberation in Catholic Thought (Maryknoll: Orbis Books, 1996).

6. See Joseph A. Fitzmyer, *Romans: A New Translation with Introduction and Commentary* (*The Anchor Bible*, volume 33 [New York: Doubleday & Co., 1993]), 610.

4. *To Hear God's Word, Face the World*

1. John Riches, *The World of Jesus: First-Century Judaism in Crisis* (Cambridge: Cambridge University Press, 1990), 1–2.

2. From *The Aprocryphal New Testament: A Collection of Apocryphal Christian Literature in an English Translation*, ed. J. K. Elliott (Oxford: The Clarendon Press, 1993), 78.

3. *The Apocryphal New Testament*, 81.

4. As quoted in Stephen Moore, *Post-Structuralism and the New Testament* (Minneapolis: Fortress Press, 1994), 89.

5. As quoted by John Updike in a book review in *The New Yorker* magazine (September 5, 1994), 102.

6. See the *Catechism of the Catholic Church* (Mahwah: Paulist Press, 1994), Nos. 2265, 2306 and 2310.

7. There is an "eschatological" dimension to Jesus' moral teaching. For example, see Wolfgang Schrage, *The Ethics of the New Testament* (Edinburgh: T & T Clark, 1988), 18–115.

8. Raymond E. Brown, *The Death of the Messiah: A Commentary on the Passion Narratives in the Four Gospels* (New York: Doubleday, 1994), volume I:165.

9. Jurgen Becker, *Paul the Apostle to the Gentiles* (Louisville: Westminster/John Knox Press, 1993), 115–116, 120–121.

10. Stevan L. Davies, *Jesus the Healer: Possession, Trance, and the Origins of Christianity* (New York: Continuum Publishing Co., 1995).

11. See John Dominic Crossan, *The Historical Jesus: The Life of a Mediterranean Jewish Peasant* (San Francisco: HarperSanFrancisco, 1991) and also his book *Jesus: A Revolutionary Biography* (HarperSanFrancisco, 1994).

12. For example, Jon Sobrino, *Jesus the Liberator: A Historical-Theological Reading of Jesus of Nazareth* (Maryknoll: Orbis Books, 1993).

13. See Marcus J. Borg, *Jesus—A New Vision: Spirit, Culture, and the Life of Discipleship* (San Francisco: HarperSanFrancisco, 1987).

14. See E. P. Sanders, *The Historical Figure of Jesus* (New York: Penguin Books, 1993).

15. Marcus Borg, *Meeting Jesus Again for the First Time* (San Francisco: HarperSanFrancisco, 1994), 119. The emphasis here is somewhat different from the earlier work.

16. See Hans Küng, *Christianity: Essence, History, and Future* (New York: The Continuum Publishing Co., 1995).

17. According to Gustavo Gutiérrez, "When all is said and done, the option for the poor means an option for the God of the Reign as proclaimed to us by Jesus." See his essay "Option for the Poor" in *Mysterium Liberationis: Fundamental Concepts of Liberation Theology*, ed. Ignacio Ellacuría and Jon Sobrino (Maryknoll: Orbis Books, 1993), 240.

18. Here I am adapting an idea which appears in an essay by Elizabeth A. Johnson, "Wisdom Was Made Flesh and Pitched Her Tent Among Us," in *Reconstructing the Christ Symbol: Essays in Feminist Christology*, ed. Maryanne Stevens (Mahwah: Paulist Press, 1993), 95–117.

5. The Place in Which We Pray

1. "To Proba, a Widow," in *Letters of Saint Augustine*, ed. John Leinenweber (Tarrytown, NY: Triumph Books, 1992), 181–182. Emphasis added.

2. On this point see, for instance, Walter Kaelber, "Understanding Asceticism: Testing a Typology," in *Asceticism*, ed. Vincent L. Wimbush and Richard Valantasis (New York: Oxford University Press, 1995), 320ff. This volume is a fascinating collection of papers. They testify to the diversity and the complexity of asceticism within the world's major religious traditions.

3. See *Towards a Society That Serves Its People: The Intellectual Contribution of El Salvador's Murdered Jesuits*, ed. John Hassett and Hugh Lacey (Washington, DC: Georgetown University Press, 1991), 285. Emphasis added.

4. I have in mind Dunne's book *The Church of the Poor Devil: Reflections on a Riverboat Voyage & a Spiritual Journey* (Notre Dame: University of Notre Dame Press, 1982). We could even include here the spirituality of non-violence espoused by Gandhi, a practice which would be inconceivable apart from a profound realization about human solidarity. Gandhi wrote: "It is the most harmless and yet equally effective way of dealing with the political and economic wrongs of the down-trodden portion of humanity. I have known from early youth that non-violence is not a cloistered virtue to be practiced by the individual for the peace and final salvation, but it is a rule of conduct for society if it is to live consistently with human dignity and make progress towards the attainment of peace for which it has been yearning for ages past." See Mahatma Gandhi, *All Men Are Brothers: Life and Thoughts of Mahatma Gandhi as Told in His Own Words* (New York: UNESCO and Columbia University Press, second edition, 1969), 90.

5. The reader looking for some concrete insight and suggestions might want to read Ched Myers, *Who Will Roll Away the Stone?: Discipleship Queries for First World Christians* (Maryknoll: Orbis Books, 1994), or Jim Wallis,

The Soul of Politics: A Practical and Prophetic Vision for Change (Orbis Books, 1995).

6. "In the cultural context a woman would rarely, if at all, claim her rights by appearing constantly, and presumably alone, in public, raising a public outcry. She also refuses to resort to bribery—a common recourse in a situation such as hers. The woman speaks of an 'adversary,' who could be an in-law....The issue is most likely a dispute over an inheritance or a dowry—that portion remaining after her husband's death." See John R. Donahue, *The Gospel in Parable* (Philadelphia: Fortress Press, 1988), 182.

7. While he provides an illuminating context for this parable, I believe William Herzog is mistaken when he claims that Luke takes the judge to be a God figure. See *Parables as Subversive Speech: Jesus as Pedagogue of the Oppressed* (Louisville: Westminster/John Knox Press, 1994), 216.

6. All Petitions Lead to the Center

1. For example, see Oscar Cullmann, *Prayer in the New Testament* (Minneapolis: Augsburg Fortress, 1995).

2. I believe this is close to what Karl Rahner meant when he wrote: "Human beings face the incomprehensible plan of their existence, which they accept as at once incomprehensible and yet as originating in the wisdom and love of God; however it may turn out, whether it brings life or death, they have a sense of themselves, with their own identity and vital impulses, as willed by God, without wanting to produce or force an intelligible synthesis between their vital impulses and the plan of their existence." See "The Prayer of Petition II," in *The Content of Faith: The Best of Karl Rahner's Theological Writings* (New York: The Crossroad Publishing Co., 1992), 518.

3. Julian of Norwich, *Revelations of Divine Love* (New York: Penguin Books, 1966 and 1982), 107.

7. Prayer and the Resurrection: Facing a World Remade

1. *Christ: The Experience of Jesus as Lord* (New York: Seabury Press, 1980), 19.

2. While I would disagree at a number of points with the approach taken by Stephen T. Davis in *Risen Indeed: Making Sense of the Resurrection* (Grand Rapids: Wm. B. Eerdmans, 1993), his book does take seriously the question "What does or should the resurrection mean to us?" For one thing, the word *resurrection* is itself already an attempt to give meaning to what happened after the cross.

3. Gerald O'Collins, *Christology: A Biblical, Historical, and Systematic Study of Jesus* (New York: Oxford University Press, 1995), 111–112.

4. The absence of eyewitnesses at the tomb site may explain why, from a narrative standpoint, the evangelists wove in the transfiguration episode. They may have realized that there ought to have been some disciples at the burial place who could testify to and describe the brilliant transformation of Jesus. Failing this, we have the earlier moment and three disciples to share it. But as spectacular as that episode on the mountain would have been, the disciples appear to have forgotten all about it; their initial reaction to the news of Jesus' being raised was one of disbelief.

5. Here I am simply following the lead of several Latin American writers. See Jon Sobrino, *Jesus the Liberator: A Historical-Theological View* (Maryknoll, NY: Orbis Books, 1993), 195–273, and Leonardo Boff, *Passion of Christ, Passion of the World* (Orbis Books, 1987).

6. My point is not that the evangelists arrived too late to enjoy an apparition of the risen Jesus, but that they had

recourse to stories in order to mediate their experience. They resonated with the imaginative world created by the Easter stories wherein Jesus actually met with, ate with, spoke with and related with his close followers. The staying power of those Easter stories consisted of their ability to evoke and clarify the experience of later generations of believers. Jesus was truly present and active among them, and their experience of his abiding presence created the possibility of their relating to the Easter stories and even imagining that the details of those stories must have happened as described.

7. As quoted in Bill Wylie Kellermann, "Resisting Death Incarnate: The Principalities of Urban Violence," *Sojourners* 25:2 (March–April, 1996), 34–37. See also *A Keeper of the Word: Selected Writings of William Stringfellow* (Grand Rapids: Wm. B. Eerdmans Publishing Co., 1994), 81.

8. Who Is In, Who Is Out: The Parable of the Vineyard

1. See D. E. Nineham, *Saint Mark* (Philadelphia: The Westminster Press, 1963 and 1977), 101–103.

2. Thomas Merton, *Life and Holiness* (Garden City: Doubleday Image Books, 1964), 41.

3. Bruce J. Malina and Richard L. Rohrbaugh, *Social Science Commentary on the Gospels* (Minneapolis: Augsburg Fortress, 1992), 133.

4. For a fascinating study, see William R. Herzog, *Parables as Subversive Speech: Jesus as Pedagogue of the Oppressed* (Louisville: Westminster/John Knox Press, 1994), 98–113.

5. Commenting on this passage in *The New Jerome Biblical Commentary* (Englewood Cliffs, NJ: Prentice-Hall, 1990), Benedict Viviano notes: "[Verse 43] is Matthew's chief contribution to the interpretation of the parable,

which in its present form is an allegory of salvation history. The emissaries are the prophets who have been killed by the people of Israel, culminating in Jesus as the son. 'Kingdom' could mean something like the present possession of God's favor and protection, but [it is probable that] it refers to the promise of the full end-time blessing. 'People' refers to the church, made up for Matthew primarily of believing Jews but also of converted Gentiles who together form the new people of God, the true Israel. This conclusion is milder than the parable; the wicked tenants are not destroyed, but the promise is taken from them" (p. 665).

6. In his book *The Gospel in Parable* (Philadelphia: Fortress Press, 1988) John R. Donahue suggests that for Jesus the parable was about the historical intensity of divine patience. The parable "summons contemporary hearers to think of themselves as the vineyard workers, confronted by a God who continually seeks them but one they can reject" (p. 55).

7. Ibid., 91.

9. The Liberation of Spirituality

1. See William R. Burrows, "World Christianity from an African Perspective: An Interview with Lamin Sanneh," *America* 70:12 (April 9, 1994), 21.

2. See Jon Sobrino, *Spirituality of Liberation: Toward Political Holiness* (Maryknoll: Orbis Books, 1988); Gustavo Gutiérrez, *We Drink from Own Wells: The Spiritual Journey of a People* (Orbis Books, 1984); Pedro Casaldáliga and José-María Vigil, *Political Holiness: A Spirituality of Liberation* (Orbis Books, 1994).

3. Gustavo Gutiérrez, *Las Casas: In Search of the Poor of Jesus Christ* (Maryknoll: Orbis Books, 1993), 459.

4. John Paul II writes: "We cannot but think of today's tendency for people to refuse to accept responsibility for their brothers and sisters. Symptoms of this trend include the lack of solidarity towards society's weakest members—such as the elderly, the infirm, immigrants, children—and the indifference frequently found in relations between the world's peoples even when basic values such as survival, freedom and peace are involved" (*The Gospel of Life: On the Value and Inviolability of Human Life* [Washington, DC: United States Catholic Conference, 1995], 17).

5. See Mark 14:36 where Jesus says: "Abba, Father, for you all things are possible; remove this cup from me; yet, not what I want, but what you want." Paul and the early communities must have picked up on the significance of this address, because Paul refers to it in Romans 8:15. Also, see Bernard Cooke, *God's Beloved* (Philadelphia: Trinity Press International, 1992).

6. The notion of the intensification of experience comes from David Tracy, *The Analogical Imagination: Christian Theology and the Culture of Pluralism* (New York: The Crossroad Publishing Co., 1981), 126 and *passim*.

7. See Abraham Heschel's remarks on the prophetic participation in divine passion in his classic study *The Prophets* (New York: Harper & Row, 1962).

8. In his book *Models of Revelation* (New York: Doubleday, 1983), Avery Dulles proposes five models which have been employed by Christian theologians. What I have proposed here is revelation neither as inner experience nor as new awareness. Jesus shared, I believe, the awareness or the consciousness of Israel's prophets, and the experience underlying his preaching was the historical experience of his people. Jesus was not a religious genius who had been gifted with a breakthrough experience or higher form of spiritual awareness. One might also want to

consult Chapter 7 of Richard McBrien, *Catholicism* (San Francisco: HarperSanFrancisco, 1994 [new edition]). What is not clear in McBrien, however, is what revelation would have meant in Jesus' case. What we think revelation is depends to a large degree on how we understand Jesus.

9. Jacques Dupuis, for example, writes: "At the source of Jesus' personal authority is a surprising nearness to God, of which the Gospel narrative has preserved striking indications. The clearest one consists in Jesus' unprecedented manner of invoking God as his Father, with the term *Abba*....It conveyed the unprecedented intimacy of Jesus' relationship to God his Father; nay more, the consciousness of a singular nearness such as needed to be rendered in unheard-of language...it testifies beyond doubt to Jesus' consciousness being filial: Jesus was aware of being the Son." See *Who Do You Say That I Am?: Introduction to Christology* (Maryknoll: Orbis Books, 1994), 49–50. As I explained, I believe that this approach is essentially guessing at language whose meaning might not be so clear as we suppose, and it does not take account of the other side of that language, namely, our relationship with God in Christ as God's daughters and sons. One wonders whether the *Abba* expression is basically christological or soteriological, whether it concerns the person of Jesus or an early experience of salvation-resurrection.

10. Keith Ward, *Religion and Revelation: A Theology of Revelation in the World's Religions* (Oxford: The Clarendon Press, 1994), 198.

11. Jerome Nadal, a sixteenth-century Jesuit charged with helping to promulgate the young Society's *Constitutions*, had a hard time with those Jesuits who could not quite let go of the traditional monastic form for shaping the interior life. "The world is our house," he used to say. But Nadal's point is applicable to the Christian vocation itself,

not just to religious life. See John W. O'Malley, *The First Jesuits* (Cambridge: Harvard University Press, 1993), 64–68.

12. *Dogmatic Constitution on the Church* (*Lumen Gentium*), No. 40. From *The Documents of Vatican II*, ed. Walter Abbott (New York: America Press, 1966), 67.

13. See *The Tablet* 247:7971 (May 22, 1993), 634.

10. The World as a School for Prayer

1. Stewart Guthrie develops an intriguing case for the claim that religion is necessarily anthropomorphic. We project human features onto our world in a multiplicity of healthy ways. His insight is especially relevant to the practice of prayer, whether we conceive prayer as addressing and being addressed (prayer as conversation) or as being known. Prayer, in other words, is going to come out of us spontaneously, provided we have not lost our ability to personalize the world. See *Faces in the Clouds: A New Theory of Religion* (New York: Oxford University Press, 1993).

2. See *The Spiritual Exercises of St. Ignatius*, trans. Louis J. Puhl (Chicago: Loyola University Press), nos. 238–250.

3. Stephen Kinzer, "Terrorized Human Tide Overwhelms Relief Camp." From the International page of *The New York Times*, Saturday, July 15, 1995. Copyright © 1995 by The New York Times Company. Reprinted by permission.

4. Nicholas D. Kristof, "The Bomb: An Act That Haunts Japan and America." From the front page of *The New York Times*, Sunday, August 6, 1995. Copyright © 1995 by The New York Times Company. Reprinted by permission.

5. Donald G. McNeil, Jr., "At Church, Testament To Horror." From the International page of *The New York*

Times, Friday, August 4, 1995. Copyright © 1995 by The New York Times Company. Reprinted by permission.

6. Kenneth B. Noble, "Thai Workers Are Set Free In California." From the front page of *The New York Times*, Friday, August 4, 1995. Copyright © 1995 by The New York Times Company. Reprinted by permission.

7. See the first two chapters of Douglas Burton-Christie, *The Word in the Desert: Scripture and the Quest for Holiness in Early Christian Monasticism* (New York: Oxford University Press, 1993). This is a very engaging study, to which I am indebted for my remarks on the emergence of monasticism in late antiquity. The reader can get a good "feel" for the spirit of the desert Christian in St. Athanasius' *Life of Antony* (Mahwah, NJ: Paulist Press, 1980).

8. In an article which appeared in 1982, Victor Codina wrote: "The first school of prayer is the muffled cry not only of the sick but also of the millions who as a social group suffer hunger, injustice, oppression, whatever their religion, creed or spiritual attitude....The poor of this world and the poor of the Church are the most authentic and evangelical school of prayer today." See "Learning to Pray Together with the Poor. A Christian Necessity," *Concilium* 159, No. 9 (Edinburgh: T. & T. Clark, 1982), 6–7.

11. The Future of Spirituality and the Option for the Poor

1. See Philip Caraman, *Ignatius Loyola: A Biography of the Founder of the Jesuits* (San Francisco: Harper & Row, 1990), 61–62.

2. See Lawrence S. Cunningham, *"Extra Arcam Noe: Criteria for Christian Spirituality,"* *Christian Spirituality Bulletin* 3:1 (Spring 1995), 6–9. See also the entry by Michael J. Buckley, "Discernment of Spirits," in *The New*

Dictionary of Catholic Spirituality, ed. Michael Downey (Collegeville: The Liturgical Press, 1993), 274–281.

3. See Peter H. Van Ness, "Practices and Meanings of Asceticism in Contemporary Religious Life and Culture" in *Asceticism*, ed. Vincent Wimbush and Richard Valantasis (New York: Oxford University Press, 1995), 592.

4. Ibid., 593.

5. See Jim Wallis, *The Soul of Politics* (Maryknoll: Orbis Books, 1995), 38ff.

6. Rick Bragg, "All She Has, $150,000, Is Going to a University." From the front page of *The New York Times*, Sunday, August 13, 1995. Copyright © 1995 by The New York Times Company. Reprinted by permission.

Afterword: Inching Toward the Year 2000

1. Paul F. Knitter, *No Other Name?: A Critical Survey of Christian Attitudes Toward the World Religions* (Maryknoll, NY: Orbis Books, 1985), 201.

2. See Matthew Connelly and Paul Kennedy, "Must It Be the Rest Against the West?" in *The Atlantic Monthly* (December, 1994), pages 72 and 76.

3. In the present work I am exploring a little further ideas I presented in *Looking for a God To Pray To: Christian Spirituality in Transition* (Mahwah, NJ: Paulist Press, 1994).

4. Alice Walker, "Beauty: When the Other Dancer Is the Self," in *Essays from Contemporary Culture*, ed. Katherine Anne Ackley (New York: Harcourt Brace, 1992), 229.